JEWELRY/METALWORK
SURVEY
#2

D0943422

A Way of Communicating

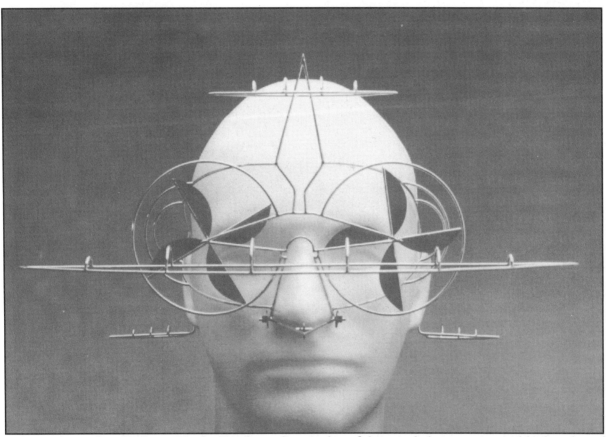

Adam Alexander Shirley, Wright Brothers Spectacles, fabricated, brass wire, gold plated and sterling silver, 5" x 10" x 5.5", 1991.

Edited by David and Shereen LaPlantz
Bayside, CA

INTRODUCTION:

Welcome to Survey #2! Our goal is still to showcase the best photos. Our definition remains as broad as possible, including jewelry, metalwork and various other materials, with many techniques. Our format remains the same, photos sprinkled amid articles by sensitive and thinking artists. I will again disappoint the critics who pounded us for not explaining why you should like/understand the art pieces. It is not for another to tell us why we should like them. Permission is only granted to the viewer by the viewer, and not ever from a second party. Freedom to choose is primary to the human spirit and creative endeavors. Without it we all loose and become prisoners. Live long and free in your thinking and your art!

DEDICATION:

In loving memory and respect for Peter Fisher whose deep abiding spirit and zest for life provided a positive role model for all he touched. His memory will spur us all to remember excellence in life and its beauty.

Publisher: Shereen LaPlantz
Editors: David LaPlantz
　　　　Shereen LaPlantz

Inquiries and/or guidelines for submitting to Jewelry/Metalwork Survey #3 should be addressed to:
　David LaPlantz
　PO Box 220
　Bayside, CA 95524
Be sure to include an SASE

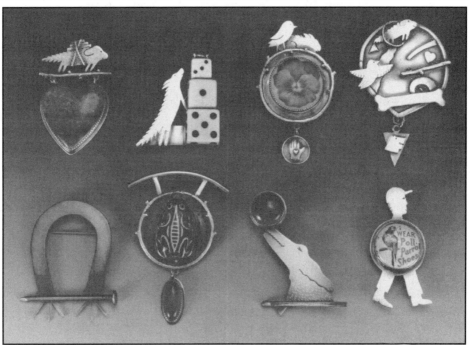

Roberta and David Williamson, Group of Pins, fabricated, cast and pierced, sterling, copper, antique dice, tin buttons, carnelian, chysophase and gold stone, average: 1.5″ x 3″, 1991. Photo credit: Jerry Anthony

Your Life Depends on This

Jewelry and metalsmithing are dangerous. Period. This book does not attempt to educate or inform you about health and safety hazards or toxic waste removal. This book attempts to inspire you; to excite your creativity. Do NOT follow any of the instructions in this book until you have educated yourself about the health and safety hazards. Your life may depend on it -or- the quality of your life. Weakening yourself, disfiguring yourself, killing yourself -or- doing any of these to someone else in your studio/home (your child?) would be horrible — it would be even worse if you did it because you were working irresponsibly because you chose not to educate yourself on health and safety.

We have included some addresses and information — just as a beginning point for your health and safety education.

The center for Safety in the Arts has numerous books and a newsletter, *Art Hazards News*. Send a LSASE for a list of publications and a sample copy of the newsletter ($18.50/yr/10 issues). Center for Safety in the Arts, 5 Beekman St, Rm 1030, New York, NY 10038 (212) 227-6220.

The Crafts Report magazine has a monthly column on health information. The Crafts Report, 800 Orange St, Wilmington, DE 19801 ($24.00/yr)

Local (see your phone book): OSHA (Occupational Safety & Health Association), NIOSH (National Institute for Occupational Safety), and the EPA (Environmental Protection Agency). There will probably be other organizations specializing in health, safety, and toxic waste removal (environment?) — don't forget your local garbage collectors, they really want you to dispose of toxic waste properly.

MSDS COULD SAVE YOUR LIFE!

MSDS = Material Safety Data Sheet. These information sheets are available from manufacturers and/or the company you purchased the product from — for each product made. In order to work more safely in you studio (office, home?) obtain and read the MSDS' on ALL the products you use. These sheets cover: product identification and manufacturer, hazardous ingredients, physical data, fire and explosion data, health hazard information, reactivity, spill, leak and disposal procedures, special protection information, and special precautions and comments.

MSDS' can be difficult to read and understand -so- contact your local OSHA office for a copy of "How to Read and Understand a Material Safety Data Sheet."

Really do it.

TOXICITY HOTLINE

For questions regarding toxicity, disposal procedures and other problems relating to chemicals in products, call the Chemical Referral Center Hotline 800-262-8200 (in Washington, DC: 887-1315). They are set up to tell you who manufactures what and how to contact them with your questions. Many of the large chemical manufacturers have a specific health and safety contact and phone number just for your questions!

ARE YOU SURE YOU'RE SAFE?

A few years ago our local garbage company sent out a listing of what was considered hazardous waste and could not be collected and disposed of by them. That list was shocking. Here are a couple of highlights:

- metal cleaners
- ammonia & ammonia based cleaners
- some adhesives & glues
- alcohols, incl. denatured & isopropyl
- epoxy paint (unsolidified)
- lacquer paint (unsolidified) & thinner
- petroleum oils & distillates
- organic solvents
- paint thinners & strippers
- silicone sprays
- turpentine & varnish

& radioactive materials like:
- some smoke alarms
- Staticmaster photo brushes

Their list is much, much longer and contains most household cleaners, automotive care products, and gardening supplies. What is this type of product doing to you if they're too toxic for a California landfill? Your life depends on your learning. Also remember it is ILLEGAL to dump toxic wastes. Have you become a small scale midnight dumper?

Your life depends on learning the proper health and safety procedures **before** following any instructions in this book.

Table of Contents

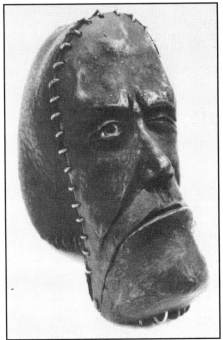

Wade S. Badger, A Mouthfull of Pennies, cast, fabricated and leatherwork, copper, silver and leather, 4" x 1.5" x 3.5", 1992. Photo credit: David LaPlantz

Note: All photo credits go to the artists unless otherwise stated.

Alan Revere

Double Diamond Earrings, fabricated, 14k gold and graduated cultured pearls, 2.5" x .5", 1992.

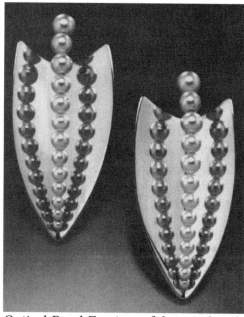

Optical Pearl Earrings, fabricated, 14k gold, platinum and graduated cultured pearls (pearls are reflected twice in the polished gold), 2.75" x 1", 1991.

Big Stars, fabricated, 14k gold and sterling silver, 2.5" x 1.5", 1990.

Photo credit: Ralph Gabriner

¿DESIGN ?

By Alan Revere

For those of us who create in the visual arts, design is a concept to be reckoned with. Whether you are creating a rocking chair, a refrigerator, a racetrack, or a ruby ring, the design of any object is an intrinsic part of its character. For some, the concept of cognitively directing the design process is unfamiliar and perhaps even uncomfortable. Yet design cannot be denied. Even an attempt to ignore design results in a design. The artist who drips paint blindly onto a canvas is intimately involved in design. Since there is no running away from design, let us explore some approaches to the process — so those who fear it will be reassured and those who love it will be stimulated to explore new frontiers.

What is design? Design is the arrangement and coordination of the parts, or details, of any object. The point of design is for the whole to achieve a certain effect or impression, or, to produce a certain result. In other words, the design of an object is the way it looks and feels, and thereby communicates a message from the creator to the viewer. Design encompasses function, appearance, composition, materials, time, space and the identity of the creator.

Four Stages of Design

The design process can be divided into: concept, development, refinement and execution. In the first stage, new and original design concepts are explored using a variety of starting points. The second stage involves the development and manipulation of these concepts into secondary concepts. In the third stage, design concepts are analyzed and refined, in accordance with your personal "rules" or standards. The best possible solutions are sought. During the last stage, final solutions are selected and finished, models or sketches of these designs are executed.

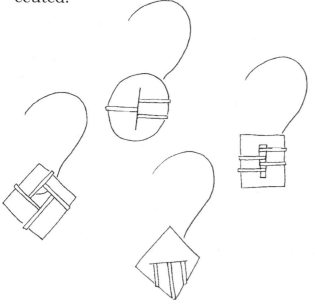

Four concepts for earrings in which one type of material is wrapped by another.

Concept

There are many starting points from which to create new designs. Sparks from a wide variety of approaches can ignite the creative fire resulting in new concepts. The wonderful thing is that different starting points result in different effects. It is a little like trying to express the same thought in different languages. A concept expressed in Japanese, German or Eskimo, will not come out quite the same as if stated in English because of the vehicle used. If you are used to communicating in one way (and are tired of saying the same thing over and over), forcing yourself to use a different means to communicate (a differ-

ent starting point for designing) will result in a surprising and wonderfully unexpected outcome. Here are a few examples of starting points for creating original ideas. They can be combined to produce a countless array of possibilities.

Materials: Begin by directly working in the material or in a substitute. Free exploration in preliminary (substitute) materials such as clay, folded paper, foil, cardboard, etc. is a non-threatening design approach used by many. Sketching ideas on paper (another substitute) is a very common, although for some, intimidating, method of designing. Some artists, on the other hand, work directly in their media, such as glass, clay, metal, fiber, etc. and just let the chips fall where they may.

Technique: Using certain processes or tools can open the door for new and exciting results. For instance, you could explore how a new or favorite tool affects your chosen material, and then study the results for clues to design possibilities. Even just sitting back and mentally exploring what would happen if you im-

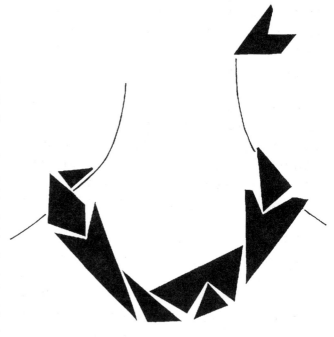

Cut paper concepts based on function as a necklace.

posed a particular action onto your material can cause insightful flashes of creativity.

Cut paper concepts based on function as a necklace.

Function: Considering the use of the object can both free, and, focus creative ideas. Function can include such parameters as utility, significance, action, display, and harmony (or contrast) with surroundings.

Personal Imagery: Dreams and internal imagery can be effective and uninhibited points of departure. Some artists literally sleep with a pencil and paper beside them, recording those midnight images unreachable during waking hours. Others employ personal narrative elements in composing a meaningful "story" as the basis of design.

Intellectual Cues: Fun and stimulating design games can be based on verbal or intellectual cues. Words like surround, explode, puncture, hide and bind conjure up images that can be expressed, developed and applied to almost any medium.

External Direction: The needs of a particular competition or a specific commission can be a forceful influence on the design process. If you were the staff designer for a manufacturing company, you might be asked to come up with concepts for twenty new products for the upcoming season. Such external pressure to produce can push a designer from behind and foster results.

Price vs Materials and Production Procedures: This can dictate the types and quantities of materials as well as the amount of labor involved in manufacture. Your design process can be focused to meet these needs.

Play: There is an endless variety of approaches to creativity. The wonderful thing about the process is, if you find yourself stuck in one mode, you can just shift gears into another. Stuck with pencil and paper? No problem, just grab some balsa wood, an X-acto knife and glue. Can't think of anything at all? Stop thinking and play with that odd tool which you haven't yet figured out completely. When it comes to being creative, don't hesitate. Don't sit around and ruminate without taking action. Follow the suggestion of the recent advertising campaign and, "Just Do It!" Because, by definition, everything you do is creative and once you start the ball rolling, momentum is on your side.

Let the juices flow: Once the creative process has begun, let it continue without abatement so that a collection of original

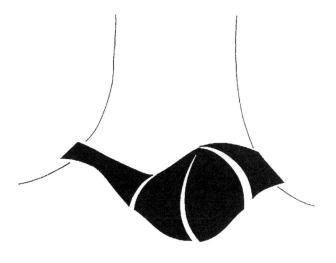

Cut paper concepts based on function as a necklace.

ideas is produced. Don't stop to admire your work. It's not yet time to focus on any one idea, regardless of how good. As soon as your "creativity faucet" is opened, let the juices flow. Use the shotgun approach and collect dozens or even hundreds of potentially usable ideas for later development. If you come up with something good, the chances are that something even better is right behind it. Think of this process as if you were taking water from a well. Whenever you dip your bucket in for new design concepts, more always fill the well waiting to be drawn up.

You are in the springtime, or planting stage, of your design concept garden. When planting a real vegetable garden, you don't just plant one tomato seed, one cucumber seed and one lettuce seed in anticipation of eating a single salad. Instead, springtime is used to plant a vari-

ety of vegetables in anticipation that some will not mature fully, and that a whole year of survival depends on what is planted in the beginning.

Development

Now that you have collected many original and innovative concepts, what will you do with them? You could go ahead and make them up into finished products without further delay. Better yet, you could invest more time in each concept, pursuing variations and developing secondary possibilities while searching for viable new ideas.

A systematic approach to developing countless new concepts: Here is a system for developing new concepts. First, always save the original. Never destroy it by working directly on it. To do so would be cannibalistic. It would be like sacrificing the past for the benefit of the present, with total disregard the future. If you want to change the design, make a tracing, a copy or a new version on which to experiment.

Close examination will reveal that each design concept is composed of details. Study it and determine which parts you like and which you would discard. Begin to think of ways to modify and improve it.

Be fruitful and multiply: Use new and original concepts as seeds for developing a new generation of variations. Keep your changes minimal. Confine them to a specific aspect of the original concept. No sweeping changes please, this is no longer the stage for pursuing completely new concepts. Instead take each original concept and create twenty new offspring, each based on a minor change. Do this for all of the original concepts you have amassed, without stopping to analyze, judge, select or reject. This process is like sampling all of the pies at the county fair

Cut paper concepts based on intellectual cues: peel (left), explode (right).

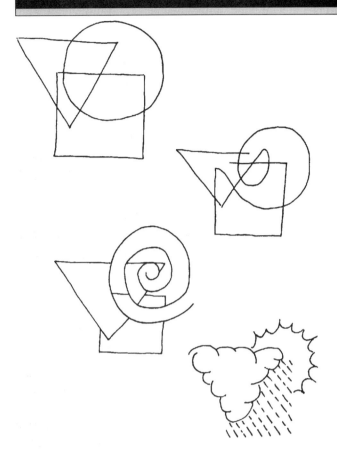

Three secondary concepts based on original solution (top left) to circle, square, triangle starting point.

before awarding the blue ribbon. In order to conscientiously complete the process, do not skip steps and jump to the conclusion that one solution is the best. However once all of the data has been collected, take your "red pencil" and put a small mark next to the ones that appeal the most.

You deserve a break: After you have created a field of new concepts, selected a few to develop, spent the necessary time expanding and developing them to a new and now larger field of solutions, it is time to rest. Step back. Take a few minutes to walk around the room, the building, the block or the universe, without bringing any baggage along. This space/time hiatus is essential to the process, because it enables you to come back with a fresh attitude for the next stage.

Refinement

It is time to return to the "drawing board," to evaluate and hone your work according to your own aesthetics. Some may argue that design is personal and subjective and cannot be discussed or evaluated according to consensus. However, a good argument can be made that there are cultural rules, or accepted general agreements by which visual designs can be measured. For the time being, at least, you are the judge, that is until you place your products in the marketplace for consumers to pass judgment. Even then, as the artist you can take or leave the consumer's decision as being either valid or invalid, as you wish.

Guidelines for refining your designs: Whether you subscribe to them or not, consider these suggestions for design refinement. Presented in approximate order of importance, these criteria can be applied to your work as well as the work of others that you view. Integrate these standards into your system for evaluating and refining designs. As you work, constantly ask yourself the questions others might ask, such as, "What is the reason the design looks that way?" "What system was used?" "Does it make sense?" "Why did the designer bother to make it?" And, most importantly, "Where can it be improved?" Look for areas of the design that do not "work." Experiment and make minor changes to improve these areas.

Be prepared to throw out all the rules: Do not place any rules above your own aesthetic. Rules are meant to be broken. We as a society would be boring and doomed to extinction if everybody followed all the rules, all of the time. However, keep in mind that rule breakers gamble and risk losing it all if they cannot successfully carry their message to the end. Creating an image contrary to all expectations can be very effective. Intentionally communicating a disturbing feeling can arouse curiosity and may be just the vehicle you need to attract attention to your message. The stakes are high, but so are the rewards.

Is the design new, original and innovative? There is no point in reproducing what has been done before. We are turned on by things we haven't seen, and, which therefore incite new responses. A design need not be totally, incomprehensibly unknown. It should, however, be different enough to grab our interest and ignite our imagination.

Is the basic concept comprehensible at first glance? It is advisable to stay within the broad range of culturally accepted and collectively experienced images so that the design can be understood. For example, eating implements fall within a limited number of styles, such as forks, spoons, knives and chopsticks. Designing a new, modern-looking fork is comprehensible, but a giant accordion-like food grabber may not be easy to relate to as a food tool. Viewers are comforted by their ability to understand the general message of a design. This enables them to focus on what is new and intriguing without the obstacles of analysis and understanding.

Does the design have an overall theme or feeling? There should be a discernible reason for creating this work. It should convey a message from the creator to the viewer. This communication, whether obvious or subtle, should be clear and justifiable.

Is there is a logic and consistency to the solution? The design should display a uniform and explainable logic system. For example, if the design is composed of straight lines and crisp angles through-

out, then there probably should not be a curved component. It just would not make sense.

Are standard shapes perfect? We are conditioned to digesting visual images in great numbers and with great rapidity. In our world of mass media and visual overload we expect certain shapes and images to be standardized. Overly complex and/ or off-kilter images that cannot be at least partially categorized immediately, leave us feeling confused. Therefore, circles should be round, straight lines should be straight, and right angles should be 90°, etc. It can be very distracting to see a not quite perfect circle or a nearly straight line. To leave them slightly imperfect results in a feeling of dis-ease in the viewer, which detracts from the message. (Keep in mind however, that it may be a justifiable goal, or effective attribute, to employ irregular and even disturbing visual components.)

Is the whole greater than the sum of its parts? This is the Gestalt Theory; that individual components, when combined and taken as a new entity, have a greater value or impact than if they were seen separately. This is the very reason for composing your design, and unless it represents something new and worthwhile, your efforts need to be re-evaluated.

Are all of the components essential? The elements of the composition should hang together with a supportable unity. If you can remove a component without destroying the design's vitality and integrity, then that part wasn't necessary. Go back and re-examine the design with an eye toward creating a totally interdependent arrangement.

Are all of the essentials present? If you can add new components, or in any way alter existing ones without detracting from the image, then again, the design was not a complete entity and should be examined further.

Are the components balanced? It is always easier to achieve balance in symmetrical designs. Radial symmetry and bilateral symmetry incorporate perfect balance due to the mirror image or star burst effect. If, on the other hand, there is no formal symmetry, components or details on opposing areas of the composition should attempt to balance each other with visual or cognitive weight.

Is the design interesting from all angles? Two dimensional graphic designs should be appealing from different vantage points. Three-dimensional designs should be interesting from all sides and all views. Good designs do not have a "backside" where the composition falls apart.

Recycle your work Once you have created new concepts, developed secondary offspring, examined, massaged and refined the results to improve the design, it may be worthwhile feeding the winners into the system for further development. Create even more offspring, again with minor variations, seeking new and improved results. Scrutinize and refine them, looking for the very best possible solutions. By recycling your work, you can create an endless stream of original concepts and develop them into a vast number of finished designs.

Execution

Sooner or later you have got to say, "Enough! Eureka, I have found it!" At this point you are ready to execute your best designs into sketches or models. You have invested your time and energy in creating original concepts, in developing variations and in refining them into the best possible designs. The products of this design system can truly be judged to be winners.

The final stage in the process is to execute accurate models and/or sketches of the best designs. These can be used to guide your creation of the actual products, to show to clients or customers, to enter into competitions, to show to the artisans who will make the final products, and as a record of your work in the future. When you have reached this point you can be sure that your designs are worthy of the time and materials necessary to bring them to reality.

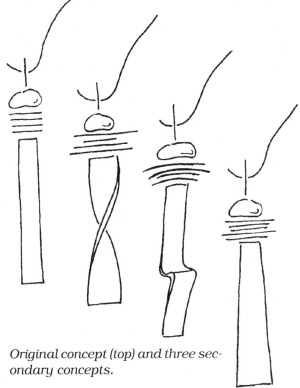

Original concept (top) and three secondary concepts.

Alan Revere is a German trained master goldsmith and jewelry designer. He is the founding director of the Revere Academy of Jewelry Arts in San Francisco and the author of <u>Professional Goldsmithing</u>. His award-winning fine jewelry is marketed through hundreds of stores and galleries across the U.S. and overseas. This article is the neculeus for a future book on jewelry design.

Hallie Katz

Pin, cast sterling silver and orthoceras fossil. The impression on top of sea snail shell is from a 340 million year old orthoceras fossil. 2.25" x 3.5", 1991.

Pendant, cast 14k gold, hessonite, garnet crystal surface, freshwater pearl. Fossil impressions taken in wax from actual 140 million year old ammonites, then incorporated into design. 2" x 1.5", 1991.

Pin: cast, sterling silver with freshwater pearl, earrings: cast, 14k gold with freshwater pearl, ammonite impression from 140 million year old fossil, 2" x 1.75": 1.25" x.75", 1991.

Photo credit: Frank Bez

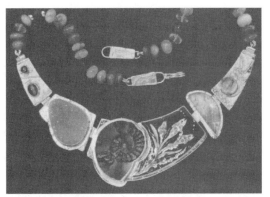

Sun Spangled, Star Sparkled, Sea Babies Swim to the Surface...Rising from the Ages, to Great the Future, enameled, fabricated and engraved, enamel, 24k, 14k, sterling silver, ammonite fossil, druzy, cocoxonite, rutilated quartz, star sapphire, tiger eye moonstone, and beads, 6" x 1.5", 1992. Copyright 1992 Marianne Hunter

Marianne Hunter

Empress Dragonfly, foil enamel with fabricated metals, enamel, 24k, 14k, aquamarine, rose quartz, diamonds, opal and baroque pearls, 2.75" x 3" x .25", 1989.

As Silks Soaked in Jeweled Hues, grisaille and foil enamels, fabricated and engraved, enamel, 24k, 14k, sterling silver, boulder opal, druzy, chalcedony, ruby, opal, lapis, and beads, 5.5" x 1.25" x .25", 1991.

Photo credit: George Post

Melissa Lovingood

Tree House, fold forming for silver, silver, red jasper and linoleum, 1990.

Abstraction, fold forming for silver, silver and acrylic, 1992.

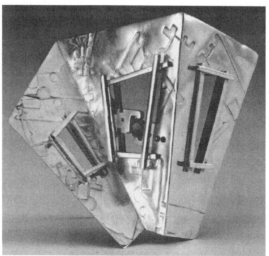

House I, fold forming for silver, silver, brass and peridot, 1990.

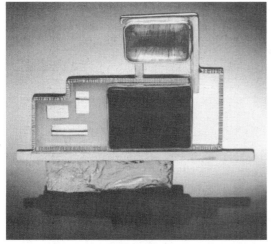

Brooch, Volumes & Voids Series #9, fabricated, sterling silver, onyx and ruitilated quartz, 2.75" x 1.25" x .25", 1992.

Erika Wolfe

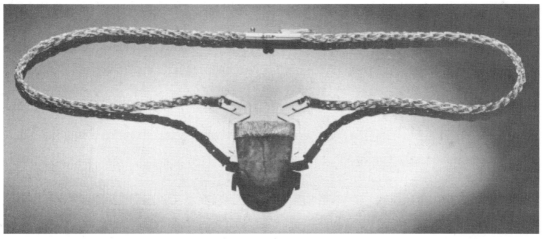

Necklace, fabricated, sterling silver and azurite, 2" x 2" x .25", 1992.

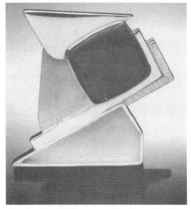

Brooch, Volumes & Voids Series #10, fabricated, sterling silver and sugelite, 1.5" x 1.25" x .25", 1992.

Photo credit: Benchmark Photography

Carrie Adell

Ancestral Echos #1, married metals, hollowformed and fabricated, shakudo, 14k, 22k, freshwater pearls and pyritize dammonite, 2" x .5" x 2", 1991.* Copyright 1991 Carrie Adell

Sedimental Blues III, hollowformed married metals, sterling silver, fine silver, 24k, 18k, 22k, shakudo and boulder opal splits, ea: 2" x .75" x .5", 1991. Photo credit: Peter Kahn Copyright 1991 Carrie Adell

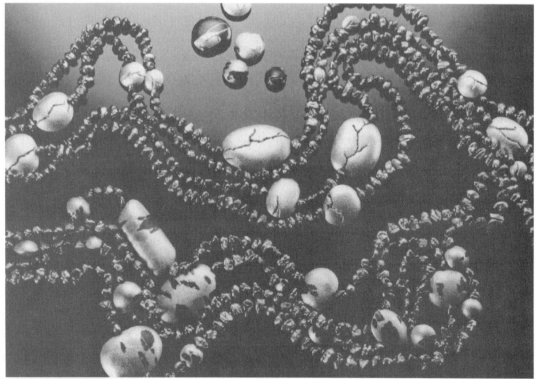

Rocks and Pebbles #2+#3, hollowformed married metals, 14k, shakudo and freshwater pearls, ea: 56" x .5" x .25", 1990.* Copyright 1990 Carrie Adell   **Photo credit: S. Deveaux*

Barbara Davis

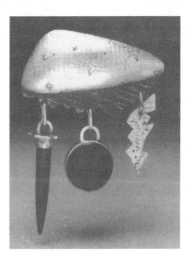

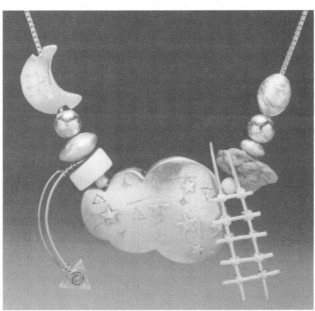

Sky Above Arizona, necklace, fabricated, hollow forms and stamp textured, sterling silver, 14k gold, marble and quartz, 24" length, 1990.*

Tribal Piece, Spirit Seeker collection, pin, fabricated, hollow forms, roller printed and stamp textured, sterling silver, matte onyx and red jasper, 2" x 3", 1991.*

Spirit Seeker collection, fabricated, hollow form, roller printed and stamp textured, sterling silver, 14k and 24k gold vermeil, and gemstones.

*Photo credit: Dean Powell

Claire A. Dinsmore

Rietveld's Plumbing: Extension, Bracelet #6, constructed and carved, sterling silver, Surell and ColorCore, 5.5" x .5" x 2.75", 1991.

Rietveld's Plumbing: Extension, Bracelet #3, constructed and carved, sterling silver, Surell and ColorCore, 5" x .25" x 3", 1991.

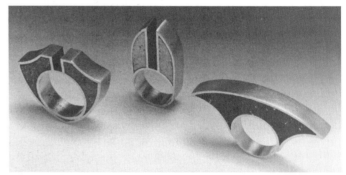

Rietveld's Plumbing:Extension, Rings #4, 5 & 6, constructed, sterling silver, Surell, Fountainhead and ColorCore, 1.25" x .25" x 1": .75" x .25" x 1.25": 2" x .25" x 1", 1991.

Rietveld's Plumbing: Extension, Bracelet #4, constructed, sterling silver, Fountainhead and ColorCore, 6" x .5" x 3.25", 1991.

Photo credit: Ralph Gabriner

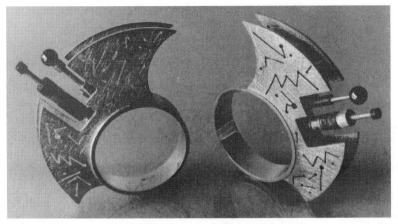

Emanuela Aureli

Towers, 2 rings, construction and fabrication, sterling silver, 18k gold, brass, copper and hematite, 1.5" x .25" x 1.5", 1990.*

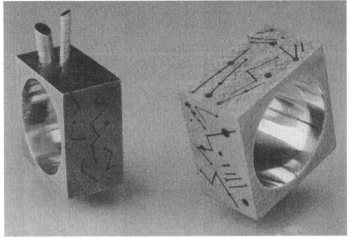

Box-Rings, construction with black patina, sterling silver and 18k gold, 1" x .75" x .5": .75" x .75" x .5", 1990.

Spirit, necklace, hollow construction with liver of sulfur, heat and patina, brass, copper and sterling silver, 5.5" longest element, 15" chain, 1990.*

*Photo credit: Ben Parrella

Harlan W. Butt

Greenbriar Series Vase #1, raising, chasing, cloisonne enamel, forging, casting and construction, fine and sterling silver, and enamel, 6" x 5" x 8", 1991. Photo credit: Brent Phelps

Harlan on Creativity

by Harlan W. Butt

Creativity, in general, you know, is kind of strange. Why do we do it? What's the point? Isn't there something better we could be doing with our time? There are many reasons for creativity, I suppose. One is a demonstration of individuality. A crying out of individual existence, a defining of oneself as separate and distinct from all others. This is no simple goal. Perhaps even more now than ever with the depersonalization of society, the reduction of people to labeled categories (consumer, yuppie, conservative, minority, executive) it's no small task to carve out, discover, or superimpose an identity on that which others see and judge as us. But on a more direct and immediate level the act of creating gives us a sense of well-being, it is satisfying to put down our mark. A signature with more universal appeal than any name.

Another reason for creativity, related to, but not identical with the first, is the innate desire for immortality. The need to manifest something that outlives this frail body and imperfect personality. Though we may publicly denounce the wish for fame, we may secretly feel that some notoriety is justified, that we deserve to be appreciated and that fame is merely an outward manifestation of recognition for being of value as a human being. And quite apart from praise is the craving to make something that is lasting.

We recognize the insignificance of our own personal being but the accomplishments of humanity (Art, Music, Poetry) go beyond the individual and are, perhaps, among the few redeeming characteristics of an otherwise rather odious and ugly species.

Creativity, on a seemingly elementary level, may be the simple need to decorate our world. Anyone who has carved a stick or painted an apartment or frosted a cake knows that there is joy in making something plain or shabby more attractive. It somehow celebrates life. It realizes some potential in an object or act. It causes us pleasure not because it is lasting or revolutionary but because it makes one moment a little better than it was or could have been.

Imposing order on a world of chaos is another reason for the urge to create. We have so little control on what happens to us and around us. We sometimes appear helpless to have even the least impression on the events that occur irregardless of our hopes and dreams. With Art we have control, if a never quite complete mastery. There is gratification in the act of causing some effect, whether fully intended or not. It can be paint on canvas, a performance on a stage, a row of umbrellas, even a photograph of a cross in a bottle of urine. It is a vision made manifest.

Another reason for creativity is release. It is a form of therapy for many, if not all who create. That which dwells inside us, sometimes wonderful sometimes nightmarish, can be brought out into the open, and even somehow shared. Anyone who has ever watched children draw knows that the results created can be delightful or horrifying. They may express glee or anguish, but seldom indifference. Somehow we can touch on that which would otherwise be too painful to mention, or too awesome to describe through our works of creative effort. The release can be ecstatic or agonizing but it is often healing. It may or may not be satisfying but it is real and can be honest and truthful and as close to a remedy for pain or an acknowledgment of joy as we can achieve on our own.

Which leads me to think that creativity is, one way or another, communication. Though the source for a work of Art may be personal and self-directed, it is ultimately an exchange, even if we attempt to deny it. Otherwise why make it manifest? Why bring it into the open? Sometimes we may be communicating privately with our inner self, but by implication, that is in a sense sharing what was previously hidden, it is relinquishing what we earlier retained. And through that sharing we become a part of the world, not aloof from or enslaved by it.

Art is, of course all these things. Sometimes it is more one than another but it is hard to see how it isn't simultaneously all of the above. But maybe it can be something else too. Just being. Birds sing with no great purpose. And it can be beautiful. The blue-gray clouds roll in and out, the thunder rumbles and spits brief rain and then the sun splits through and the thin oaks cast cool stripes across the warm ochre surface of the dry winter grass. For no reason. No justification needed here. The dogs range and root, they eat my garbage and poop in my yard. And it's great. Because it's just that. Enameled bowls and hammered metal rods pose in a gallery and in my studio and on some shelf. I look at them with awe and some detachment. The white bits of paper are lying on the ground amidst the orange rinds and egg shells. It really is wonderful somehow. But I better go now and pick them up.

Born in Princeton, NJ, Harlan completed degrees at Tyler School of Art and Southern Illinois University. He has been Coordinator of Jewelry and Metalwork at the University of North Texas for the last sixteen years. A metalsmith, enamelist and poet, he has combined ecological concerns and Buddhist philosophy in his work since 1972. He lives in Denton, TX with his wife Pip and his two children, Falkner and Jaclyn.

Mizusashi #1, raising, chasing, enameling and construction, copper, enamel and silver, 6″ x 6″ x 9″, 1990. Photo credit: Brent Phelps

Kiff Slemmons

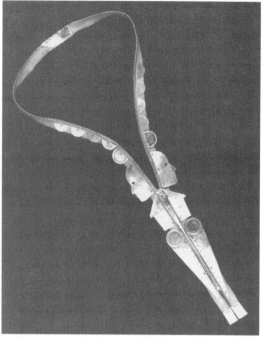

Romance, cut engraved and sewn, brass and zipper, 17" x 2.25" x .5", 1991.

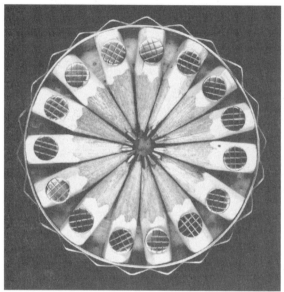

Pencil Pie, fabricated, silver and pencils, 2.75" x .25", 1991.

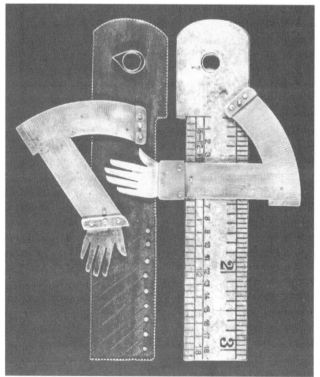

What's Your Angle?, fabricated and riveted, silver, copper, brass, ebony and ruler, 5" x 4.25" x .25", 1991.

Roberta & David Williamson

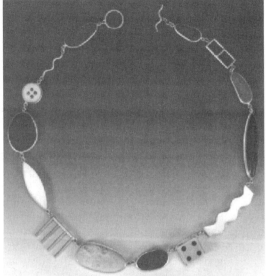

The Four of Us, fabricated and pierced, sterling silver, beach stones, antique dice and button, 26", 1991.

Photo credit: Jerry Anthony

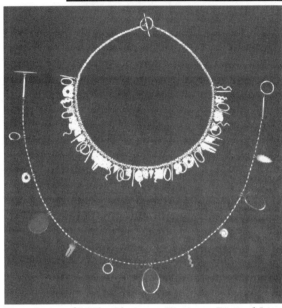

Top: Lots of Little Charms, Bottom: Dotted Line Necklace, pierced and soldered, sterling silver, bronze, 22k gold plate and beach stones, T: 22" B: 26", 1991.

Good Citizen, fabricated, sterling silver, antique dice, tin buttons and stone, 7.5", 1990.

Betsy Douglas

Pewter Cups, scored, folded, fused, fabricated, file finished and gold plated, pewter and sterling silver, 2.25" x 2.25" x 3.25", 1989.

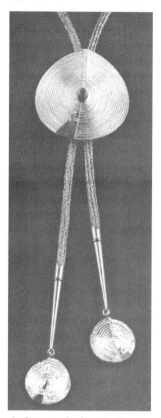

Ashante bolo, Ashante lost wax casting, fabricated and crochet chain, sterling silver, 14k gold, bi-metal (18k and sterling), fine silver and rutilated quartz, 2.25" disk, 38" chain, 1992.

Vessel #1 - Folded Form Series, scored, folded and fabricated, pewter, 3.5" x 4" x 6.75", 1989.

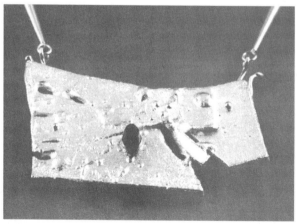

Rock Explosion Pendant - Ashante Series, Ashante lost wax casting, engraved, forged, crochet chain and granulation, sterling silver, 14k gold, invicolited tourmaline and fine silver, 2.5" x 1.75" x .25", 1992.

Photo credit: Bill Douglas

Kenneth C. MacBain

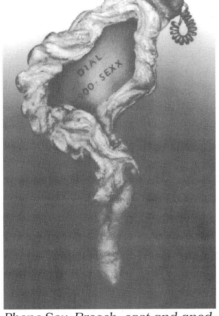

Phone Sex, Brooch, cast and anodized aluminum, 4" x 2.5" x .5", 1991.

Untitled Vessel, mokume gane, anodized aluminum and steel, 7" x 3" x 3.5", 1991.

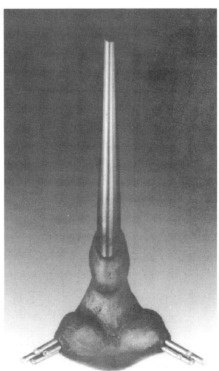

Untitled Brooch, cast and anodized aluminum, and steel, 4.25" x 2.25" x .5", 1991.

And Now A Word From Our Sponsors, Brooch, cast bronze, 3.5" x 2.5" x .5", 1991.

Personal Viewpoint

by Duffy Franco

RICE and BEANS

1 -16 oz. can kidney beans
4 Tbsp. vegetable oil
1 medium onion, chopped
Tabasco sauce
2 cloves garlic, chopped
1 1/2 cups uncooked rice
1/2 tsp. oregano
1/2 tsp. chili powder

Prepare rice according to directions on box. In skillet sauté onions, garlic, oregano and chili powder in oil until onions are translucent. Add beans with half the liquid drained off. Simmer gently, stirring occasionally for 15 minutes. Serve over rice with Tabasco sauce to taste. Contemplate happiness.

The above recipe is furnished for metalsmiths and all artists who subsist on incomes similar to mine. Why do I find myself eating this so often? Because I'm making the jewelry I want to make. Not designs that follow the latest trends, not rings clipped out of department store catalogues, not commissions designed by customers. My jewelry.

You see, I have ideas in my head. Visions. Forms that excite me. When I pick up a pencil to sketch I'm trying to imprison on paper an elusive sensation in my mind: the sensation of something that's "right," that clicks. It may be a junction of two shapes, an angle that is pleasing, perhaps a certain mechanical function. I know it when I find it.

How, when after so many pages of sketching, do I know I've hit on something? Because it's perfect. I begin to get excited, to smile inside. I've projected this vague ghost of an idea with pencil onto paper. It's got a name now, a shape. It's been captured; now I can make it.

Understanding this whole process of searching and discovery, let's compare a different approach: picking up a fashion magazine to see what's hot. Seeing what the Celebs are wearing. Watching TV. Using the media and the market as a basis for your jewelry designs. Suddenly your work is being based on someone else. It becomes derivative of what a person or group of persons feels, thinks, or wears. And your work is a part of a whole trend of design that will soon pass. You deliver to the public what they expect; hence they get nothing unexpected. Creativity halts at the point a piece bears resemblance to all the other objects on the market. Everything becomes a knock-off of everything else.

I refuse to get caught in that circle. By ignoring the fashion magazines, the public and the prevailing trends I allow myself quite a bit of elbow room. Suddenly I've got flexibility, true originality and purity of design. I'm not being influenced by what Oprah has on. When the fashion winds blow my way and work starts selling fast, great. That's a wonderful feeling. But I'm not going to attempt to chase those winds when they change direction. I've got a direction of my own.

Commissions also fall under the category of work based on someone else. If someone designs a piece for me to make I'm being hired solely as a mechanic, to give shape to their ideas. But suppose I don't like that idea? Suppose I think it's gruesome? Do I sign it? Let them tell their friends I made it? I know there is personal satisfaction for some jewelers in fulfilling someone else's dreams, but I have too many dreams of my own. Selfish, but true.

Most of my time at the bench is spent making my production line. Pieces I know intimately. Yes, I can procrastinate, yes I get bored working at times, but when I'm at my best I feel truly inspired. I see more.

There is a pleasure, a working spirit found in picking up the right tool and affecting the metal with it. "Tools are an extension of the hands" I recall one teacher saying. Pliers, hammers, files and the torch, all play a role in the ballet of force that creates a piece of jewelry. My bench becomes a landscape. Tools fall where hands drop them, scattered in rank of need emanating from the center, where the piece lays being filed, examined, and worked.

When I pull the finished piece from the warm sawdust, dry and polished, and lay it down on a cloth I enjoy looking about, seeing all the tools at rest, some powerful, some delicate, each one having contributed a part in the creation of something so beautiful and precious. It is as if the piece has a whole history the customer will never see.

When all of my work comes together in my booth, under the lights and arranged just so, this is where the public interacts. Some pass by, others linger only briefly. But then there are the few that stop, look at it all, then look again. They see a difference from other work. They ask questions, admire, and try things on. Then they buy it. They trade their hard-to-come-by cash for something I've made. That makes me happy because I know they're happy, that they really mean it, they understand what I'm saying within the context of my work. I've communicated non-verbally with someone through shape and form.

It is a small section of the market that buys my work. I don't make a lot of money from my jewelry, but it's what I want to be doing. I'm happy. I do a little substitute teaching here and there to make ends meet. I always get by.

In a craft trade journal I saw an ad directed at buyers. It was for these small, furry, large-eyed ceramic creatures available in uniforms of various professions. The one pictured was a fireman. The copy read, "Designed to fire up your sales." We had the rice and beans last night. It really tasted good.

Duffy Franco began making jewelry in high school around 1976. He later attended Catholic University in Washington, D C. Realizing jewelry is what made him happy, he transferred to Tyler School of Art in Philadelphia, where he graduated in 1983. Franco has been doing craft shows since 1986. He presently resides in Norwalk, CT.

6" x 4" dia.

The Glasnost Egg

by Frank Trozzo

We had little idea what we were getting into when commissioned to make a Faberge style egg. The idea was exciting! We dove into the project without realizing the manpower, time and expense that go into such an endeavor. Sometimes you have to make something first to learn how you would never do it again. Some projects seem to go on forever. This was such a project. No matter how much work was done, it felt as if this project would never be completed. The deadline came and we delivered it on time. The five of us who worked on it day and night for four months were happy to see it go, exhausted, yes and very proud.

The Aurum Glasnost Egg was a homage to the fall of the Iron Curtain and the opening of Russia. We were fortunate to have had Edward Osetchkin, a visiting Russian goldsmith to help with the design. It took ten ounces of 18 Karat gold, 100 ounces of sterling silver, five carats of diamonds and countless hours of work.

The body of the egg was lathe spun. The dimensions were done on computer. Then they were sent by fax to the spinner who made the top and bottom forms over which the spinning would take place. We chose sterling silver for strength. Fine silver would have been a better choice we later learned.

The egg was spun in six parts. First, a layer was spun of 1.2mm sterling silver sheet for the enamel base. Then a 1.2mm copper sheet was spun over the sterling, followed by another layer of heavier sterling, 1.5mm thick. The three layers were heated to separate them. The copper served as a spacer for the enamel layer. The copper was then put aside and the four silver parts were cleaned. The two heavier silver halves were cut out in the style of a basket. The models for the gold panels were made from the pieces cut from the silver. Under the interlacing panels there are sunburst patterns engraved and filed into the metal body of the egg. This caused the light to undulate and reflect through the enamel. The technique is known as *basse taille* (French, "low-cut").

The next step was to assemble the egg and prepare it for enamel. We chose to attach the interlacing gold panels to the egg itself, and not to the outside basket. The egg was prepared with small spacers to keep the panel's pins from touching the enamel and causing fractures. The golden panels were cast and finished. The complexity of the panels made it difficult to mold and cast. The finishing required two skilled engravers.

While the panels were being prepared the enamel was ground from lumps, washed and applied. Two layers were fired and then ground with diamond files, filled and refired. The first half of the egg fired without incident. The second half lost a large section of enamel in the first firing, causing us untold difficulty with fire scale and discoloration. This is why fine silver would have been better than sterling.

Once the firing had been done we assembled the egg. The original plan was to solder the pins holding the panels with soft lead solders. Instead, we opted to use a system similar to that used on sailboats for cleating lines. For the final assembly, we invented a spring rivet that curled tight and kept the right amount of pressure on the assembly.

The surprise inside was an enameled sculpture of a child. This is not pictured because it is a corporate logo, and the owners request that it remain anonymous.

> I have been creating jewelry for twenty years now, and learning something new each time I sit down to the bench. I sit at the bench nearly every day for practice if nothing else. My studio is my business. I enjoy the camaraderie of others, and I also enjoy commerce. We work in a traditional venue, and we provide services to our customers.
>
> My work is traditional in technique. The inspiration comes from mythology, history and nature. I like to do things with a twist, if possible, an ingenious variation.

Interchangeable Necklace and Bracelet, 50ct amethyst, 4.65ct diamonds, 18k yellow gold and pearls, 1991. Copyright 1991 Frank Trozzo

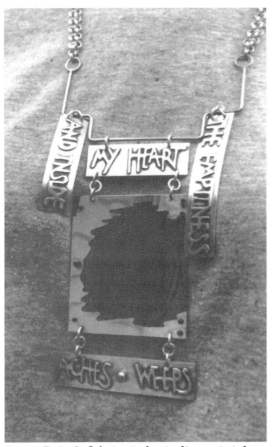

Love; Pain I, fabricated, sterling, stainless steel, chrome-plated steel, Xerox on colored film and brass bolts, 6.5" x 3.75", 1992.

Fiona Maclean

Entrapment, forged and fabricated, sterling, copper and patinated copper, 3.25" x 4.5", 1989.

Photo credit: Glenn Sheller

Billie Jean Theide

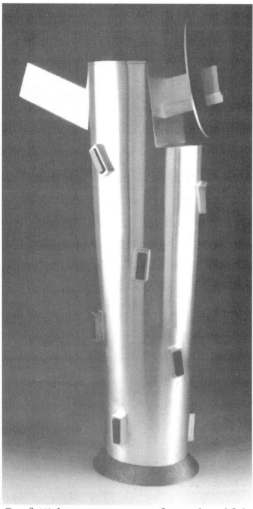

"S" Brooch, fabricated, aluminum and sterling silver, 5.75" x 1.75" x .25", 1989.

Confetti, beverage server, formed and fabricated, sterling silver and aluminum, 6" x 4" x 12", 1990.

Swimming Swan, teapot tea infuser, formed and fabricated, sterling silver and aluminum, 5" x 1.5" x 5", 1991.

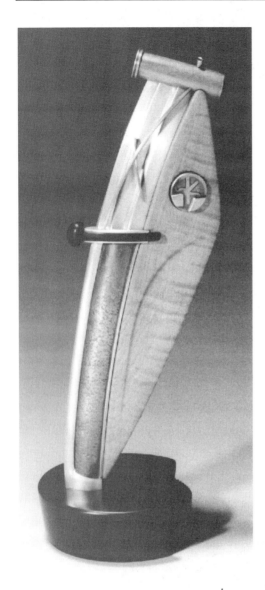

Joe Muench

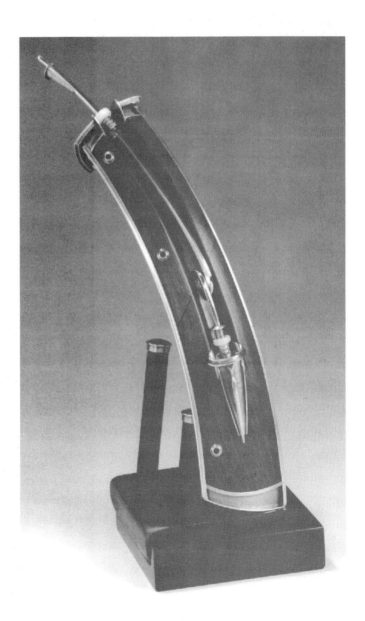

Kissaki, fabricated, formed and carved, sterling silver, stainless, brass, copper, nickel, acrylic and wood, 3.5" x 3.5" x 10.5", 1991-92. Copyright 1992 Joe Muench

Even Steven, formed, fabricated and carved, sterling silver, 14k gold, acrylic, nylon, wood and slate, 6" x 6" x 13.5", 1991-92. Copyright 1992 Joe Muench

Photo credit: David Kingsbury

Marcia A. Macdonald

Solitaire, spun, pierced, carved wood and fabricated, sterling silver, walnut and door knob plates, 14" x 14" x 9", 1991.*

Contained Series, 3 brooches, soldered and fabricated, sterling silver, rusted steel, brass, copper and broom straw, ea approx: 4.5" x 1.25" x .25", 1991.*

*Photo credit: David Brown

Lydia Anne, stamped metal, fabricated and carved wood, sterling silver, fork, antique iron, brass, paint, steel, copper and wood, 16" x 3.5" x 7", 1989. Photo credit: Susan Hamlet.

Frederick Jon Marshall

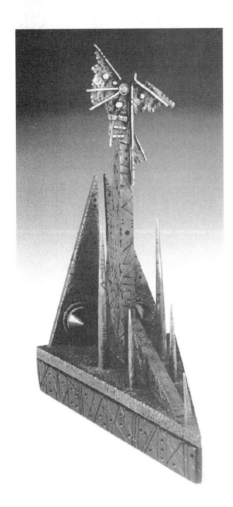

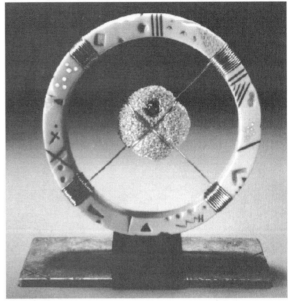

Ring of Wisdom, sculpture/bracelet/brooch, fabricated, carved and electroformed, 14k, 18k, fine and sterling silver, copper, brass, ivory, ebony and tourmaline, 4.75" x 1.75" x 5.25", 1990.

Temple Guardian, sculpture/ brooch/earrings, fabricated, carved and fused, brass, bronze, copper, sterling silver, onyx, wood and amethyst, 8" x 3", 10.5", 1989.

Photo credit: Ralph Gabriner

Safe Haven, sculpture/brooch/bracelet, fabricated, cast, fused and carved, copper, brass, bronze, nickel, vermeil, wood and semi precious stones, 7" x 7" x 4", 1989.

Leslie Ewing

Dora Maar, urn, fabricated, sterling silver, copper and glass, 4" x 3" x 5.25", 1992.

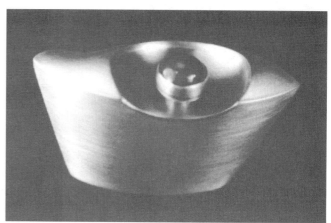

Window of the Soul, perfume bottle, fabricated, sterling silver, copper, glass and carnelian, 2.5" x .5" x 1.25", 1991.

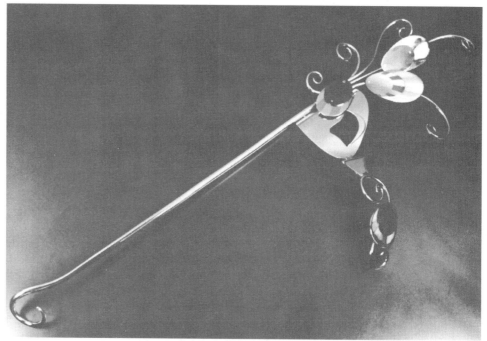

Photo credit:
Bryan Huntley

Untiled Mask, marriage of metals and hot forged, sterling silver, nickel, brass and niobium, 22" x 8.5" x 2.5", 1989.

Trudy Borenstein-Sugiura
Frances Bregman

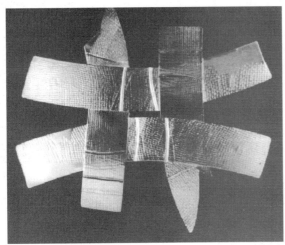

Trudy Borenstein-Sugiura, New Calligraphy #2, fabricated, sterling silver, 3" x 3", 1990.

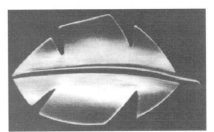

Trudy Borenstein-Sugiura, Banana Leaf, fabricated, sterling silver, 2" x 2.5", 1991.

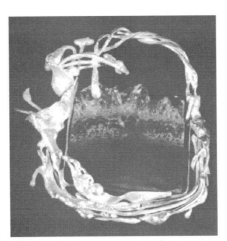

Frances Bregman, Basket, pendant/brooch, fabricated and fused, sterling silver and agate, 2" x 1.5", 1991.*

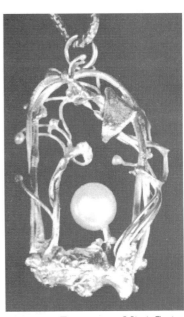

Frances Bregman, Mini-Gate, pendant/pin, fabricated and fused, sterling silver and cultured pearl, 2" x 1", 1991.*

*Photo credit: Menlo Camera

Frederick Wm. Scott

Travelin' Lite, sheet construction and stamping, brass, copper and nickel, 3" x 1.5" x 1", 1991.

Photo credit: Doug Koch

Chiggers Memorial, stamping, repousse, roller print, inlay, enamel and forging, nickel, copper, sterling and enamel, 9' x 5" x 2", 1990.

The Eagle Flies on Friday, stamping, repousse, roller print and sheet construction, copper, nickel, brass, sterling, bronze, glass and paper, 10" x 6" x 1", 1990.

Songbird Resolve, sheet construction, repousse, piercing, stamping and roller print, copper, bronze, sterling and feathers, 14" x 8' x 3", 1991.

Jennifer Swartz

Hearts of the Pure, fabricated and painted, wood, paint, leaves and brass hinges, 3" cube, 1991.

Life as a Visionary, fabricated and painted, wood, lens, paint, film, mirror and brass hinges, 3" cube, 1991.

Photo credit: Davo

Tears of the Disenchanted, fabricated and painted, wood, paint and Xerox, 3" cube, 1991.

Linda Hesh

L'Amour Fou, pin, casting and construction, silver and garnets with 14k catch, 2.5" x 1" x 1.5", 1991.

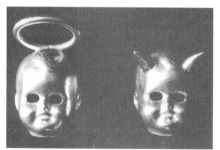

Good & Bad Babies, earrings, cast silver, 1" x .5" x .5", 1991.

Bed Bug, pin, casting and construction, sterling and 14k bugs, 3" x 1.75" x 1", 1991.

Curtis K. LaFollette
Aimee Krzyscin

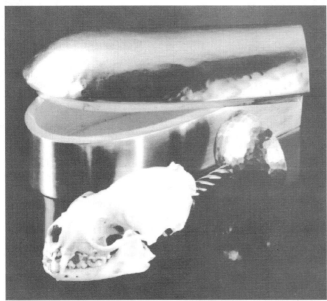

Curtis K. LaFollette, Euthanasia Set, fabrication, sterling silver and skull, coffin size: 5" x 2.25" x 2.25", 1990. Photo credit: Nash Studio.

Aimee Krzyscin, Box #1, fabrication, casting, sandblasting and oxidizing, silver and copper, 2.5" x 1.5" x 1.5", 1992.

Lotte Cherin

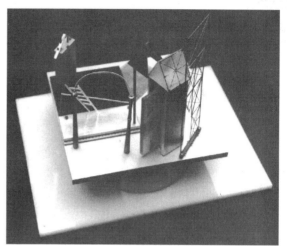

Dream Castle, cast and fabricated, acrylic, brass, aluminum, copper and laminates, 6" x 6" x 6", 1989-92.

Untitled with Rings, fabricated, aluminum, steel and copper, 13" x 12.25" x 2.5", 1991-92.

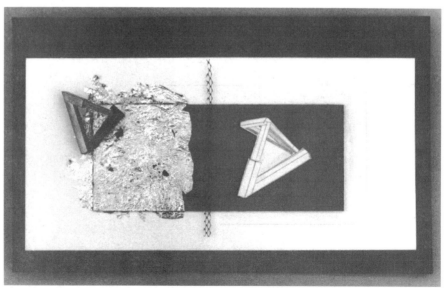

Untitled, fabricated, gold leaf, brass, paper, graphite and plastic, 10" x 1" x 5.75", 1991.

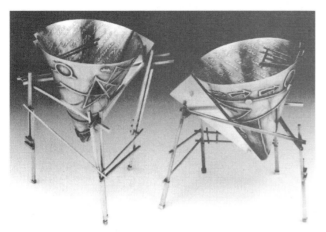

Linda Darty

The More the Sun Shines, fabricated, etched and enameled, sterling and enamel, 10" x 7" each, 1991.

The More the Sun Shines, fabricated, etched and enameled, sterling and enamel, 10" x 7", 1991.

The More the Sun Shines, fabricated, etched and enameled, sterling and enamel, 10" x 7", 1991.

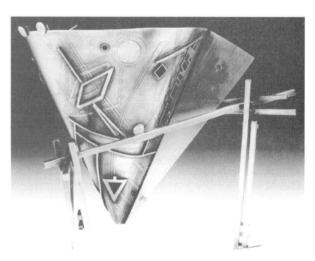

The More the Sun Shines, fabricated, etched and enameled, sterling and enamel, 10" x 7", 1991.

Photo credit: Phil Burzynski

Cuttlefish Casting

by Chuck Evans

Cuttlefish are of the mollusk family, along with oysters, squid, snails and clams. The cuttlefish has 10 cephalopods or tendrils similar to its relative the squid, but it also has a calcified internal shell that the others do not. It is the internal shell, or bone, that has washed on to seashores for thousands of years. Most of the bone's structure is relatively soft, but brittle, one side very soft and the other layered with a thin almost transparent hard cover.

At some point hundreds of years ago metalworkers began using the soft side of the bone to form ingot molds. Eventually the soft sides, or let's say the faces, of two bones were made flat, a cavity carved into them, a pour opening formed and the two pieces bound together to create a mold. Later it was discovered that relatively hard objects could be pressed into or between the faces leaving an almost exact impression or negative shape of the object. Almost exact, except for the texture of the bone's striated internal structure. This texture is made up of alternating layers of hard and soft calcium. The texture was undesirable and eventually metalworkers began using various compounds to coat the interior mold surfaces providing a smoother surface. Some continued to pour into untreated molds and simply filed or stoned the cast piece smooth. Cuttlebone is still used today in some cultures for ingot molds. The workers then file off the texture prior to processing the raw ingot.

Through all the centuries' metalworkers have used cuttlebones I can find no evidence that it was ever used artistically for its unique textured structure. Until the early 1960's when the Italian brothers and goldsmiths/sculptors Gio and Amaldo Pomodoro explored its textural possibilities. This surprised me considering how long our ancestors had been using the material. My introduction to the technique was as a student in the late 1960's

Each person must decide for themselves how safety conscious they will be. This article shows one artist's approach to their own studio work. Do not follow it vervatim -- decide for yourself on the important issues of health and safety. See page 3.

of Professor Albert Paley at the School for American Craftsmen. Just a few years earlier Paley and his classmates had been taught the technique by their teacher, Professor Stanley Lechtzin at Tyler School of Art. At about the same time they discovered the Pomodoro brother's work shown in <u>Modern Jewelry An International Survey</u> by Graham Hughes. I believe these two factors resulted in, perhaps the first significant artistic use of the process in this country. For a brief period cuttlebone casting was relatively popular. But interest in it has faded along with cast forms overall.

I began using cuttlebone again for a brief time in the early 1980's as background research for a book. In hindsight, my coverage of the subject was as superficial as all others since Herbert Maryon's <u>Metalwork and Enameling</u> of 1912. In 1990 I was asked to demonstrate the technique as part of a workshop series in Kofu, Japan. The workshop participants were all prototype makers or designers working in Japan's commercial jewelry industry. I was surprised they had requested the topic. I had assumed they were well versed in the process since Japan is the major exporter of cuttlefish bones. In fact, the cuttle I pre-shipped to Japan had originated there. The workshop went well. The participants seemed amazed and taken with the process and results. In less than two days one company had used their prototype maker's workshop sample to develop a rubber mold and prototype earnings in 18 karat yellow gold with diamonds!

Prior to the Japan trip I started using a few cuttle castings that I had done years previously and had put aside in my junk/tech sample drawer. My renewed interest was stirred by several factors. I wanted to be as proficient as I possibly could, so it would at least appear to the Japanese that I knew what I was doing and could be of service to them. Coincidentally I became intrigued with the results of altering the raw castings in the rolling mill or with hammers. The almost accidental results, and the spontaneity of the whole process, is exciting. Aside from all that, the technique is low tech and inexpensive. Large (7"-8") cuttlebones purchased in quantity cost me about $.30 each. The casting requires some metal, a torch, crucible with handle, and the bones.

Those who have experienced this process must have noticed how clean and almost scale or oxide free the castings turn out. This interested me also, since it is difficult to do consistently clean, scale free castings using other types of casting methods and mold materials. Most investment or mold material incorporates elements that contribute to oxidation and scale. Cuttlebone does not. Cuttlebone is almost pure calcium. As the molten metal goes into the cuttle mold, the calcium on the mold's surface decomposes into calcium oxide to form nature's almost perfect casting environment. Calcium oxide, a near

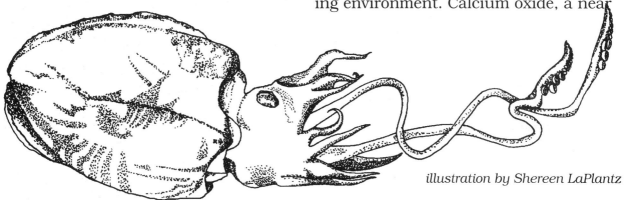

illustration by Shereen LaPlantz

ideal molding material, is commonly used in metallurgy research and development.

The Process

Select two bones close in size, length and width. You'll notice one side is pure white and soft (the face) and the other side much harder, brittle and shell-like (the back).

Exposed back edge is clipped away.

Using diagonal pliers, clip away the back edge of both pieces to make the back edge flush to the outer edge of the front. Be careful handling the bone, its brittleness causes it to break quite easily. It is important that this edge be trimmed flush in order to be able to flatten the faces completely.

The quickest and most effective way I've found to flatten the faces is to carefully rub them over a section of clean, flat, poured concrete, as on the patio, loading dock, sidewalk or over the side of a concrete block. The traditional method of rubbing the two bones together to do the initial flattening takes too long, makes a dusty mess in the studio and often results in cracked or broken bones. The bones are fragile, especially to the inexperienced. As they are rubbed in a circular motion over the concrete use the full hand on the bone to give an even, gentle pressure downward over the entire bone. A belt-sander will of course do the same job, but not all have this luxury or want the dusty mess in the workspace.

Rubbing the faces flat on the concrete only takes a few seconds. As you rub notice the sound and feel as the soft material of the face is abraded. When the face is nearly flat the feel and sound will change as the outer edge of the harder "back" material comes in contact with the concrete. Stop now, and again clip away the newly exposed hard edge around the bones. Take the two, face to face, between your hands and gently rub them together for just a couple of seconds. This final "clip and rub" will make the pieces perfectly flat, creating a good seal.

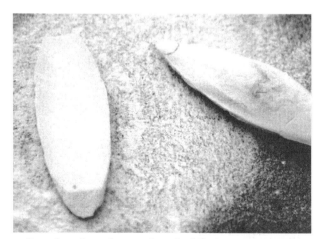

One face has been abraded flat over concrete.

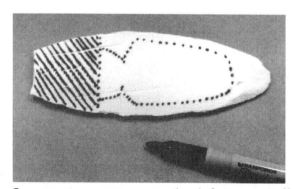

One-quarter section, on the left, is cut off. Dotted line shows pour opening, mold area and outer sealing surface.

Now plan how large (length and width) a mold area you will need for the finished casting, plus the height and width required for the sprue or pour opening. I prefer a wide, short pour hole into the mold. This provides a better pour target and is direct. Remember in planning the mold and sprue area to leave sufficient sealing surface all around both regions to retain the metal as it is poured in.

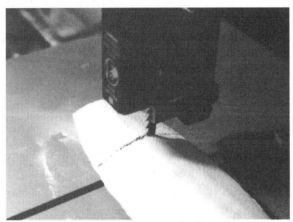

Section is cut off using the band saw.

The remainder of the process; designing and making the mold area, venting, setting up for the pour and the actual pour are essentially the same as described in most current textbooks, except for a couple of things. In cutting off approximately the top 1/4" of the bones along the top edge of the sprue opening, I recommend a fine to medium tooth bandsaw as opposed to the jeweler's saw. Using a jeweler's saw is cumbersome and often causes the bones to break. Hold the two pieces together face to face, rest the bone on the saw's cutting table and cut through both in one careful pass across the blade. If the pieces are prepared as outlined, binding wire is not needed. A strip of masking tape wrapped around the bones near the top and bottom is quite adequate. The tape is easy to apply and less likely to contribute to breakage, as is often the case with binding wire.

I am certain that my most recent experiences with cuttlebone will lead me to experiment with new ways of using this unique material. Some attempts have been made to do vacuum and centrifugal assisted cuttlebone castings. The realization that calcium is an almost perfect environment in which to pour metal leads me to ponder why commercial casting investment manufactures cannot develop a higher quality product. More questions arise, but I'll save those until next time. Good luck with your castings.

The Rest of the Process Illustrated

A spoon can be used to carefully scrape out a pour opening in both pieces.

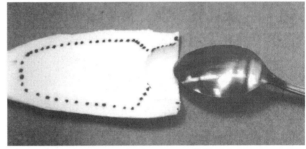

Useful tools for impressing, cutting or scraping the design.

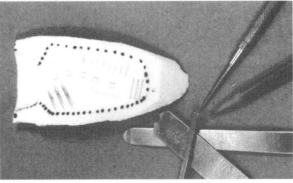

Design and tools used.

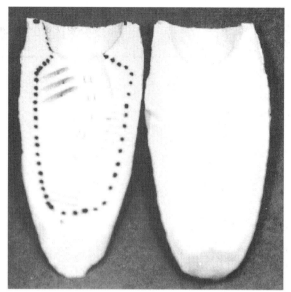

The two pieces ready to go together.

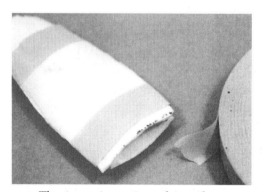

The two pieces taped together.

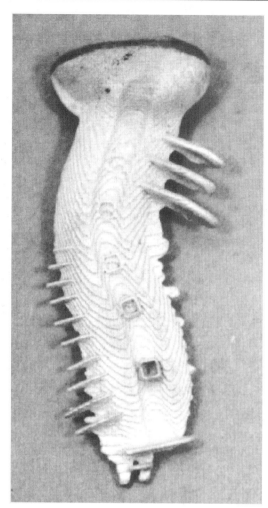

Just out of the mold.

The cuttlebones set in a pan to catch any spilled metal. Casting crucible and tongs.

Chuck Evans received his MFA from the School for American Craftsmen in '72. Until '78 he taught at Bowling Green State University, when he moved to teaching at Iowa State University where he is still. His strongest compulsions as a young kid were to be a sailor, paint and draw, and build hot rods. The least desirable task was to sit for hours in the boring, uninspiring class rooms of North Carolina's public schools. After ten years he threw in the towel and spent ten years in the Navy. From there he ended up in Rochester, NY and the beginning of what he does now. There were also five poorly crafted hot rods along the way. I also owe much gratitude to many fine people who have helped me along my way.

Chuck Evans

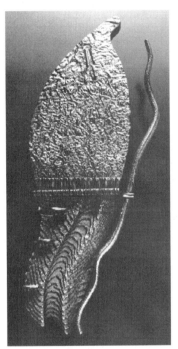

Can't Help It If I'm Lucky, cast and constructed.

If You Gotta Go, cast and constructed.

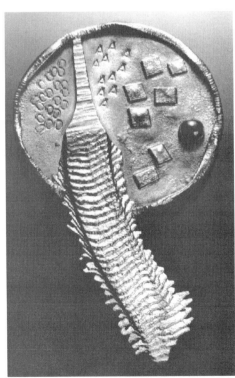

I'm Just Bleedin, cast and constructed.

Last Thoughts of Mexico, cast and constructed.

A.C. Racette
Nancy Shapiro

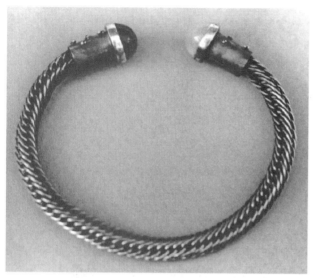

A.C. Racette, Arm Cuff, Latvian wire twisting, granulation and construction, bronze, fine silver, blood stone and moonstone, 3.5" x 2.5", 1992.*

Nancy Shapiro, Pin and Earrings, cuttlebone casting, sterling silver and zebra jasper, 3" x 1.5": .5" x 2", 1991*

Nancy Deal
Jan Krenke Southern

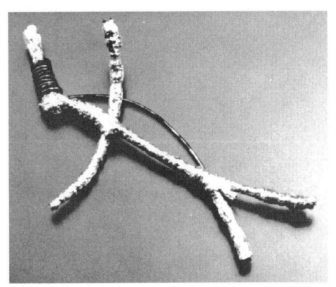

Jan Krenke Southern, Stick Fetish, wrapping, sterling silver and niobium, 3.5" x 2.5" x 1", 1991. Photo credit: Brian Huntley

Nancy Deal, Rings, constructed, sterling silver, moonstone and hematite, 2" x 1" x 1": 1.25" x 1.25", 1991 and 1992. Photo credit: Nancy Shapiro

Donald
Friedlich

Interference Series Brooch, carved, roller printed, riveted and fabricated, slate, 18k gold backed with sterling, 2" x .25" x 1.75", 1991.

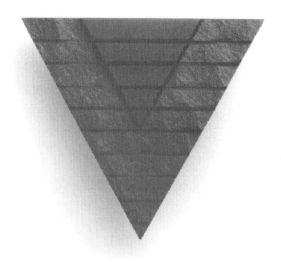

Interference Series Brooch, carved, riveted and fabricated, slate backed with sterling, 2.25" x .25" x 2.25", 1992.

Interference Series Brooch, carved, roller printed, riveted and fabricated, slate, 18k gold backed with sterling, 2" x .25" x 2", 1991.

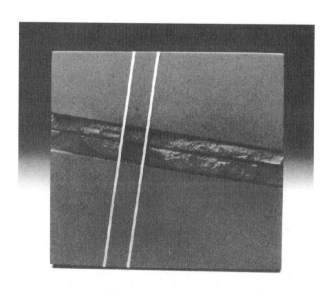

Interference Series Brooch, carved, inlay and riveted, slate, 18k gold backed with sterling, 2.25" x .25" x 2", 1991.

Photo credit: James Beards

Valerie Davisson

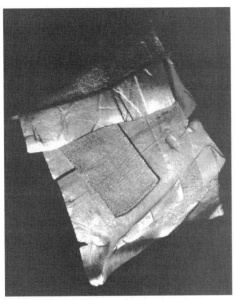

Untitled, fabricated, folded and roller printed, sterling and fine silver, 18k and sterling silver laminate, 2.5" x 2" x .5", 1991.

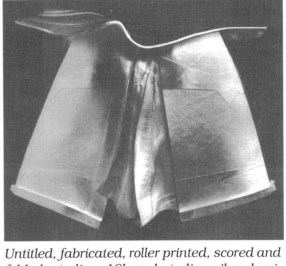

Untitled, fabricated, roller printed, scored and folded, sterling, 18k and sterling silver laminate, 2.5" x 3" x .75", 1991.

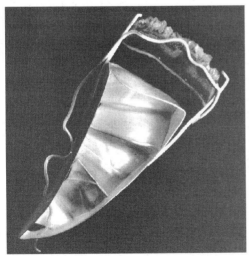

Untitled, fabricated and folded, fine and sterling silver, and tourmaline, 4.5" x 2" x 1", 1991.

Untitled, fabricated and folded, fine and sterling silver, and antique Chinese jade, 4" x 4" x .75", 1991.

Photo credit: Gary Valiere

Pat Davis Candler
Virginia Causey

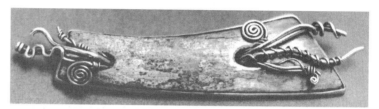

Pat Davis Candler, Mammoth Dreams, brooch, fabricated, sterling silver and mammoth (fossil) ivory, 4" x 1.5", 1991.

Pat Davis Candler, Composition #3, pendant, fabricated, forged, reticulated and fused, sterling silver, fine silver and black onyx, 1.5" x 2.25", 1991.

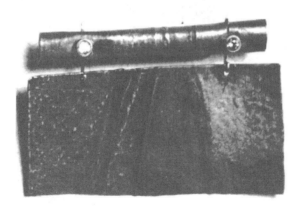

Virginia Causey, Textured Pin, folded, roller printed, tube set and heat patinated, sterling silver and citrine, 1" x .25" x 2.75", 1989.*

Virginia Causey, Series I Pin, roller printed, folded, cold connected and heat patinated, sterling silver, 14k and tourmaline, 2.25" x .5" x 1.5", 1989.*

*Photo credit: Jerry Arthurs

Barbara McFadyen

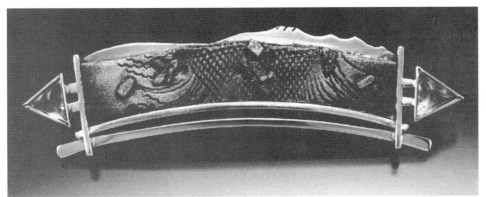

Torri Gate, brooch, fabricated, enamel, sterling silver, 14k and 18k gold, copper and aquamarines, 3" x 1" x .25", 1989.

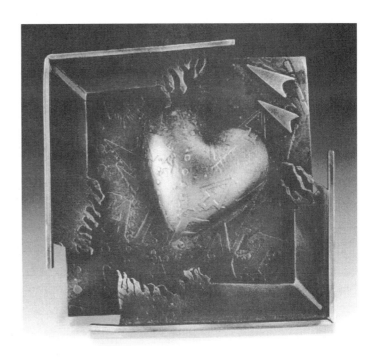

Untitled, etched and fabricated, 14k gold, sterling silver and brass, 2" x 2" x .5", 1990.

Photo credit: Ralph Gabriner

Judith Bettencourt

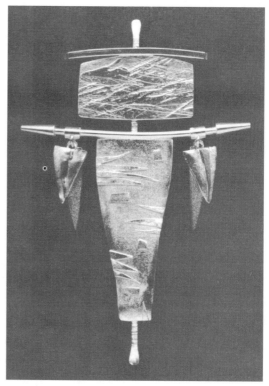

Bangkok Bound, fabricated, fused and etched, sterling silver and 18k gold, 4" x 2.75", 1991.

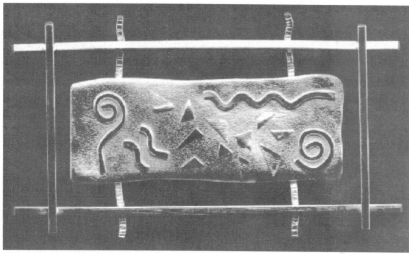

Thai One On, fabricated and fused, sterling silver and 18k gold, 2.75" x 1.5", 1991.

Photo credit: George Post

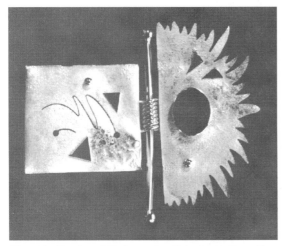

Lisa Jean Wade

Kinetic Series #1, brooch, fabricated, reticulated, pierced and hinged, sterling silver, 14k yellow and red gold, and turquoise, 1.75" x 1.5", 1991.

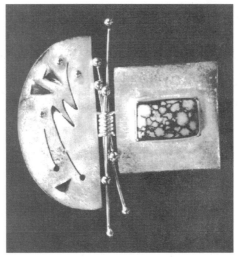

Kinetic Series #2, brooch, fabricated, reticulated, pierced and hinged, sterling silver, 14k yellow and red gold, and Chinese turquoise, 1.5" x 1.75", 1992.

Kinetic Series #3, brooch, fabricated, reticulated, pierced and hinged, sterling silver 14k yellow and red gold, and lapis lazuli, 1.75" x 2", 1992.

Domed Earrings, fabricated, reticulated, pierced and domed, sterling and 14k yellow and red gold, 1" x .5", 1991.

Photo credit: Jon Van Arsdale

People Are Things

by ROY

Playwright Edward Albee said, "People are things," at a lecture in Pittsburgh. It struck a note. He was born a playwright, he said, and added, "Fortunately, I like what I do." For me it is the same, except I work with metal.

Art, I think, is created from a unique energy and a need to communicate — visually. It is more communicative than any language. With this energy for creating, the artist can build a technical vocabulary quickly and apply it to the concept. The excitement can be shared: It does not matter which gender, or the number of artistic participants.

"Do women have difficulties being taken seriously in art?" Of course: That is why the question is often asked. Possibly, my working with metal is a reason I touch on this topic. People have been amazed that women can successfully perform the techniques using power tools, torches, hammers and saws.

Artists living and working together can travel a road to happiness. It is hard to imagine one making art, even collaborating. If artists can cut loose their grip on ego, then collaboration can be the most creative experience. Boris and I have been working individually and collaboratively for seven years. Our completely different styles and ways of interpreting help us to share thoughts. An invented metal shape by one may find its way onto another's work. We inspire each other. Singing and dancing to blaring music in our studio is common (much to the surprise of our Polish Hill neighbors). Swearing over firescale and a slipped file is a typical commotion. Being ripped happily away, while working on a piece, to see another's is part of this energy. Together, we combat the dreaded artist block. When one is down, the other is up, keeping our motivation on fast-forward.

The art intensity is high and exciting in our studio.

continued on page 64

The Metals Addict

by Boris Bally

Our studio, the second floor of an old warehouse, consists of a special focal point: The jewelers bench with two stations. Working here with ROY, my wife and partner, I am happy. This environment is under control. Although, it is true, the medium of metal remains unpredictable: I feel drugged. We are art junkies.

But we are not alone. A web of similar addicts are connected globally through faxes, phones, letters and miscellaneous vibes. We communicate with quickened pulse, slurred speech and anxious gestures. Excited tips and short-cuts of small metal feats and adventures are eagerly shared. Sometimes we leave our metal-dusted, dark-cave studios to meet. We even form networks for support: We can not miss a fix: We will not let another addict miss a fix.

So many years we have waited and prepared for this moment at the bench. Past mentors' words whisper to me: "You can do anything if willing to trust yourself....analyze objects, environments, situations, always trying to improve them...do the best you can... work hard and you will overcome all obstacles... be a positive thinker." Years of technical information massaged into me. Always wondering where the long-drawn technical focus would lead. The technical has become the words for my poem.

Now, finally, I can begin to regain the innocence of freedom. The best way to learn has been to make mistakes, sometimes on purpose, and laugh at the results: The crash course method has been my best teacher.

The letter eagerly ripped open: The phone receiver quickly replaced. An offer! A jubilant battle shriek! An Irish jig: I recognize another potential fix. The project is presented, debated, juried, officiated, financed and organized. Papers pass the details and signatures through the skies. A deadline has been set for the delivery, opening, showing, publicity, reviews, traveling and returning. The piece, which does not even exist yet, has been spoken for.

Goals and inspiration swell at the bench

continued on page 65

Brainstorming begins when we focus on a theme, material, process, or deadline. Collaborating involves a lot of give and take. On occasion, one person has a stronger "vision" of what the end result should be and refuses to act on input. Fortunately, this creates a positive competition and ideas continue to soar and circulate. They eventually prove themselves.

Collaborations inspire future or ongoing artwork, whether it be joint or individual. The cycle of ideas, creativity and imagination sprout from everywhere: environment, people, architecture, art, dance, design, music...etc. A collaboration, I feel, is a direct influence from another creative person.

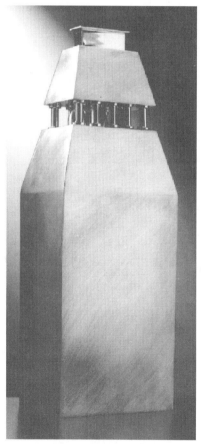

Temple of Three Eggs, designed for "Fortunoff Silver 3" exhibition, cast eggs, fabricated, silver and gold eggs, 11.5" x 3" x 4", 1991. Photo credit: Dean Powell.

Often, I am asked, "Where do ideas come from?" There are no formulas. But Ben Shahn, painter and author of <u>The Shape Of Content</u>, believed life experiences and surroundings were keys to inspiration. Read this book! (Published by Harvard Univ Press, Cambridge MA & London, England, 1957.)

Impact: When I was pounding the New York City pavement, gallery to gallery, seeking the "art answer," Ivan Karp, (Director of OK Harris Gallery, NYC:) said, "Impact! Impact! That is the solution!" Again, there are no secret ingredients to finding the power of *impact.* If for one second, I can make a viewer lose themselves in my work, something has been accomplished. They can contemplate lives, beauty, form... and my work is given importance.

When I *sketch,* ideas flow. One work leads to another, each art piece is a study. Pre-drawing is not always necessary, because I do not know exactly what will happen to the composition in its final stages anyway. Sometimes it becomes more important, if the work involves precious materials and possible financial waste.

Risk taking is always paramount. If one is feeling too comfortable, it's time for change. Change, however is difficult to accept because it means one has to get uncomfortable.

When I *hit* on a design or concept I like, it is a personal victory. If it becomes a limited edition, it is the musician who sings a song over and over, hoping to fine-tune the results. When a piece *fails,* it must fail GLORIOUSLY.*

A Studio-Sketchbook Thought...6/22/91: Art reflects the artist. Be off the edge to be "cutting edge." The fever to create an art piece is a microcosm of the art world

continued on page 66

— a flurry of ideas whirling, pushing and advancing to the fingers. Sometimes I must sit still a moment to regain priorities. The best way to begin a project is: To begin. (Otherwise I'll try to postpone the euphoria by doing all the unimportant things I can think of.)

The drug of inspiration has come from the decaying urban surroundings of this industrial-age sleepy-town. Also, I have a need for technical challenge, and the mysterious desire to wage a battle between the boundary of safety and danger.

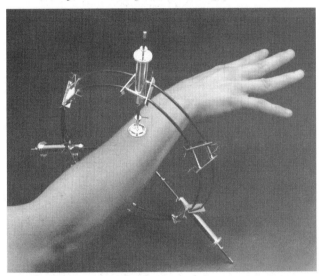

Constrictor Armform, fabricated, tube settings, spring mechanism in cylinder, "twist" cold-joined closures and rivets, silver, rubies, stainless steel, oxidized brass and titanium, 2" x 11" x 11", 1990. To wear form, push pistons out (rubies move out), insert hand and allow pistons to "grip" wrist. Photo credit: David L. Smith.

The needle is inserted:
An idea-
quick scheming-
pencil sketch-
crumpled and tossed... Stop! (become
     unsure) ...make a
paper model: change this-change
     that...rip it apart-
select material
turn-up the music and the bass !
BEGIN and COMMIT !

The rest becomes automatic. A manic fury, the project becomes excitingly numbing. It becomes the focus and problems fade. Sometimes I can feel an inner rhythm and understand the reason for existence. The pulse balances. An angry piece can become a peace-maker: My hands forge a gun barrel into a feather!

A piece emerges from the bubbly veil of ammonia water — it is patted dry. I awake to reality a hundred hours later. When was this object made? How did it happen so fast? Where did the ideas come from? Was it difficult? I rub my eyes...

Sometimes this cycle takes days, or weeks. The main focus during these times is the project in hand. Like a junkie with a need for a fix: I will not let anything interfere

When the high drifts away, the need for responsibility returns: A name must be given. A description; a weight; the measurements. Photos must be made. They become the only evidence of this mysterious birth of the new piece: We become proud parents who have photos of our children hidden in their wallets to remind themselves they do have kids — although they are grown-up and have gone away to college.

Surprisingly, the "hands on" work has given way to more office work than I ever imagined. I am learning to plan my time better, to maximize the results of the creative work rush. Studio-time has become my *fix*. What was once a self-motivated frenzy, has now become a goal induced pace. Years ago, opportunities were always self-made, with much effort and time, and seldom promised this rush. Now, happily, fixes come frequently and there is much less fear of withdrawal symptoms setting-in.

This cycle breeds an optimism which I

continued on page 67

disease. Little fevers in different parts of the world create an entire chill. comes and goes...temperature waves appear very suddenly then disappear. left only to the memory. Making art history.

Creativity and originality grow from within the individual male or female. Technique, can be learned. Art has no rigid guidelines.

*words of mentor and friend, professor and artist, Douglas Pickering.

Boris Bally and ROY met at Carnegie Mellon University where they both graduated with BFA's in 1984. In 1986 they founded 2D3D Studio, and are currently self-employed crafts artists. They lecture about inspirations, their work (RISD, Parson's, Edinboro, Public High Schools). Boris taught foundation design at CMU (1989-91). ROY is teaching metalsmithing at the Pittsburgh Center for the Arts. Both were featured in the Fortunoff exhibition: "Silver: New Forms and Functions." Other shows include: "10.Silbertriennalel,"

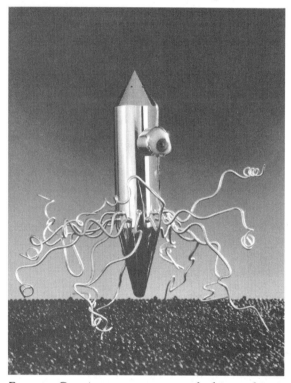

Pepper Crustacean, pepper shaking object, designed for "10 Silbertiennale" exhibition, Hanau, married metals, fabricated and riveted, silver, oxidized brass, gold, prosthetic eye and labradorite, 9" x 10" x 10", 1992. (Pull out the eye to fill with pepper and expose the labradorite stone.)

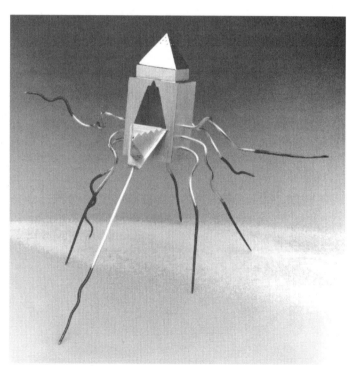

Salt Crustacean salt shaking object, designed for "10 Silbertiennale" exhibition, Hanau, married metals, cast, fabricated and hinged, silver, oxidized brass and gold, 8" x 8" x 6", 1991. (Stairs fold out to fill with salt.)

Photo credit: Dean Powell

Hanau, Germany; "Borne with a Silver Spoon," curated by Rosanne Raab; "Art That Works," curated by Lloyd Herman; "More Than One: Studio Production," The American Craft Museum, NYC. Morrison-Rink/Precious Metals Gallery, in Portland, OR will be hosting a two-person exhibition, November 1992. Collections include Torsten Bröhan, president Gesellschaft für Goldschmiedekunst, Germany, and Indiana Univ. Art Museum. Their works have been featured in Product Design 3, Contemporary Crafts For the Home, Vogue, Pronto.

must eagerly share with beginning metals students: I have felt the rush, now to deal the addictive drugs of the metalsmithing trade. Yet, in the corners of red eyes I can see shadows of our possible pit-falls and hard times. We have tried to prepare for them. They will come. But we remain addicted to this art-lifestyle... and optimism will push us through.

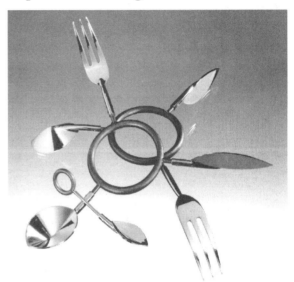

Eat Wear, wearable placesetting, cast, fabricated and file-textured rivets, silver and gold plated brass, 10.5" x 11" x 1.5" (bracelet), 1991.

Decision T-Pot, designed for "10 Silbertiennale" exhibition, Hanau, fabricated, silver with gold plated interior, 16" x 16" x 6.75", 1992.

Photo credit: Dean Powell

Jon
Havener

Whisht, bronze, 28" x 26" x 23", 1991.

Whirlpool, bronze, 30" x 30" x 30", 1992.

Photo credit: E.G. Schempf

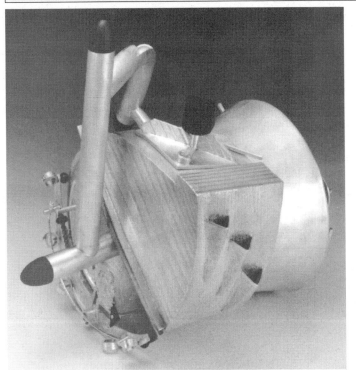

World Tea Time, tea server with 2 detachable brooches, cast, fabricated, etched and roller printed, 18k gold, sterling, ebony, baroque pearls, hematite and yellow jade, 11" x 8" x 9", 1990.

Vernon G. Theiss

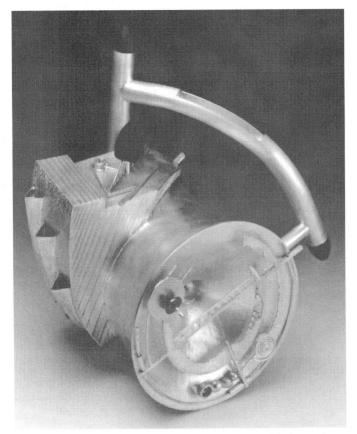

World Tea Time, tea server with 2 detachable brooches, cast, fabricated, etched and roller printed, 18k gold, sterling, ebony, baroque pearls, hematite and yellow jade, 11" x 8" x 9", 1990.

Lois-Diane Frankel

Potpourri Container, assembled, perforated steel, brass and iron, 5.5" x 2.5" x 3", 1991.

Potpourri Container, assembled, perforated steel, brass and iron, 7.5" x 2.5" x 3.5", 1991.

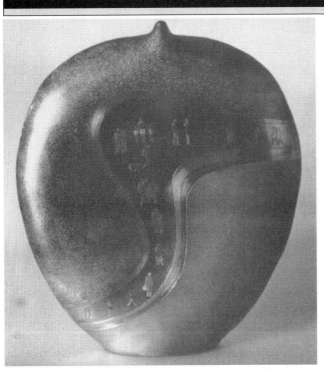

Life Parade, etched and fused, pewter, 8" x 9", 1991.

Claire Pfleger

Lightning, etched and fused, pewter and aluminum, 8.5" x 11", 1990.

Allen
Perry

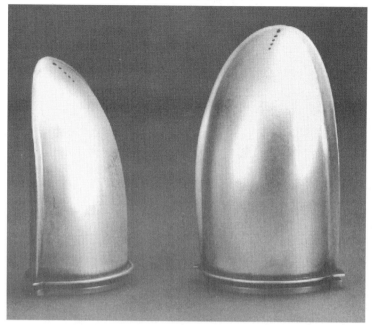

Salt and Pepper, die formed and fabricated, sterling silver, 3", 1990.

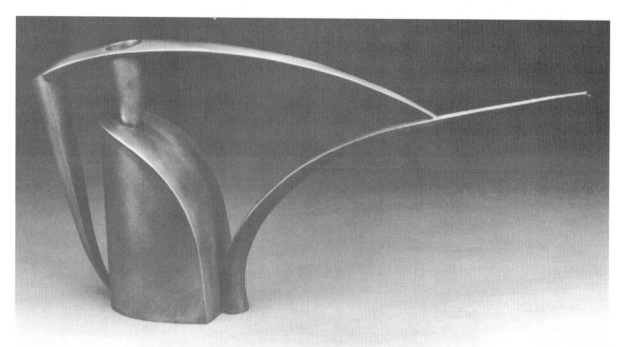

Watering Can, fabricated, bronze, patina, 30" x 7" x 14", 1991.

Photo credit: Andrew Edgar

Megan Corwin
Ronald Wyancko

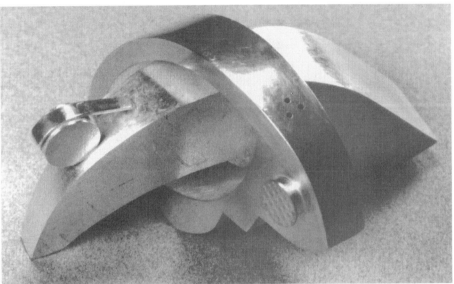

Megan Corwin, Salt Piercing Pepper, salt and pepper shakers, fabricated, sterling and 18k gold laminate, 5" x 1.5" x 3", 1991. Photo credit: Constantine Sparis

Ronald Wyancko, Bowl, raising, shell forming and forging, sterling silver, 8" x 6" x 6", 1992.

Brigitte Clavette

Decanter, fabricated, copper and amethyst, 1.5" x 8.25" x 9", 1991.

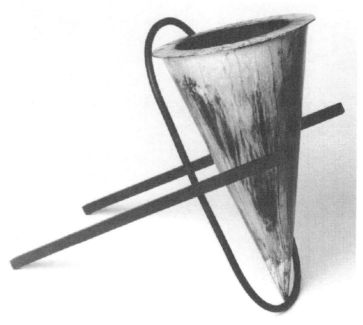

Untitled, fabricated, patinated and painted, copper and gold leaf, 10" x 10.5", 1991.

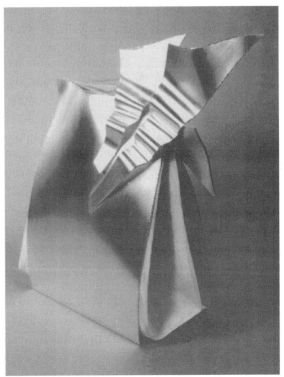

Whispers, fabricated and folded, sterling silver, fine silver and fabric, 6" x 2.25" x 7.25", 1992.

Barbara Nilausen-K

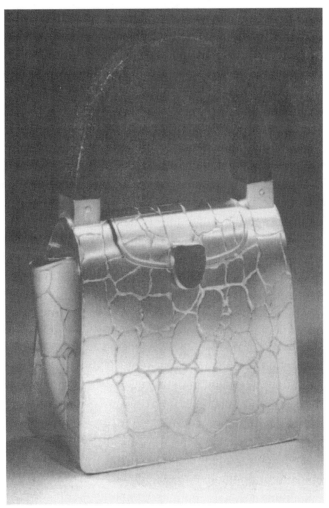

Alligator Teapot - Tea For Few, fabricated and engraved, sterling silver and cortan, 5.5" x 2.5" x 8", 1991.

Lucinda Brogden
Karen Miller-Thomas

Lucinda Brogden, Relay of Fear, chased, bronze, pewter, faux marble and a steel saw blade, 12" x 12" x .75", 1991.

Karen Miller Thomas, Al-E-Fuser, tea infuser and stand, fabricated, brass, sterling and lapis, 7" x 2" x 2", 1991. Photo credit: Jerry Anthony

Traditional Silversmithing Repousse/ Chasing

by Ron Brady

We met by chance in Acapulco and Ricardo Lopez de Grado changed my life.

In truth, I first met wife Teresa when she graciously offered to help me translate something from Spanish. This led to a pleasant conversation about many things but, as we talked, I became increasingly fascinated by the large ornate medallion she was wearing. I had never seen anything like it before. To me it was it was a piece of ageless beauty, crafted I knew not where -- but I had to find out. Teresa said her husband made it and asked if I would like to meet him. I did.

He was a Spanish master silversmith, heir to a family tradition reaching back through many generations, faithfully passed on from father to son. It is called repousse and chasing, and those who are willing to dedicate their time and effort to its considerable demands are rewarded with products of classic beauty.

Ricardo was naturally pleased with my interest in his work. He patiently answered all my questions during the rest of our vacation in Mexico. But the more I learned, the more questions I had. It eventually became clear to us that I had much more than a passing interest in Ricardo's art.

When it came time to leave Acapulco, we decided to remain in contact. I was invited to their summer home in Rome, NY for a week. Thus began my career in the practice of this little known art.

A Whole New World

Working with Ricardo over the years opened a whole new world within me. It was a world that went well beyond the ordinary things, like the mechanics of crafting a silver medallion. Indeed, I sometimes felt I was caught in a time warp. For example, Ricardo spoke very little English, and I, almost no Spanish. Yet it was easy for us to communicate with each other, even on the most intricate process details. Sometimes Teresa would translate for me, but somehow I already grasped what he had said.. Surprised, she would ask, "How did you know that? From a purely rational point of view, I still don't understand it.

Perhaps this is what classic art is all about -- the ability to communicate without words. After all, much of our knowledge about past civilizations, going back thousands of years, comes not strictly from translating their writings. Beyond mere words lies the rich treasures that archaeologists have discovered within the ancients' paintings, their architecture and all of countless artifacts that dazzle the eye and teach us. We know of their culture, their values, their beliefs and their life styles mainly through the art they left behind.

Ricardo taught me to appreciate that classic art has the power to free us, not only from the bounds of language, but also from time. And geography. And political boundaries. And so many other fences that too often keep us apart.

Herein lies the joy in working with silver. This is my justification for all the time, effort and dedication it takes to produce a work that meets both Ricardo's standards and mine. I will never know the final resting place of my carefully crafted pieces, nor the journey they will take to get there. But I can imagine! And this is what makes it all worthwhile.

Money? Of course it's important and I value it at much as anyone, but I see no good reason to make it into a limit, another fence beyond which I will never travel. Pride in my work, and the idea that I may bring joy to those not yet born, is the bonus that defies any price tag. It provides all the incentive I need to continue my work with repousse and chasing.

The Birth of a Design

All manner of things influence my designs. Since a child, my sketching and doodling would be scrolls, swirls and intri-

Hummingbird pendant, repousse and chasing, sterling silver, 3.75"H. This is my version of the medallion which Teresa wore when we first met.

cate designs. This, of course, is where traditional silversmithing is best utilized. My designs are influenced by nature, architecture and stone work on buildings, both new and old.

Lately I find I am very influenced by Art Nouveau and Chinese designs. I do not care to make a "museum reproduction" in total. I lean toward traditional designs, predominantly Spanish, which was what so attracted me to Ricardo Lopez de Grado's work when I first met him.

I allowed myself the luxury of learning by my mistakes, working solely in brass for

Each person must decide for themselves how safety conscious they will be. This article shows one artist's approach to their own studio work. Do not follow it verbatim — decide for yourself on the important issues of health and safety. See page 3.

four years, so that I never worried about ruining or wasting a piece of silver. I never strove for that "magnificent piece of work" in the beginning. Instead, I was much more interested in learning technique and the making of tools. And as many aspects as I could absorb from working with Ricardo while watching him at work.

Today I must have at least 800 repousse and chasing tools. However, if I want to achieve a specific result, I will stop and make the tool, rather than settle for something else. Compromise is a stranger to quality.

My techniques employ the use of a pitch pot almost all the time. The only time the pitch pot is not used is; when forming the shape of the vessel (bowl, plate, basin shape, etc.) and when finishing (straightening, polishing and uniformly finishing the entire piece).

In describing the process the following terms will apply:

Melted Pitch: Pitch softened until it is the consistency of warm taffy.

Repousse: Working from the reverse side or back.

Chasing: Defining and finishing of the front or viewing side.

I start with a disk of 20 or 22 gauge in sterling or fine silver. I then raise the metal into the desired shape of the project.

The Process

Repousse

After the plate has been annealed, the edges are crimped down with a pair of smooth pliers. Then the plate is filled with melted pitch, including any flat sections up to the crimped edges. The pitch pot is prepared with a flat bed of 1 1/2" to 2" of hardened pitch.

Melted pitch is poured into the pitch pot (about 1/2"). Then the silver is placed into the softened pitch and pushed down until the pitch comes up and around -- but not over -- the edges of the silver. (Water and wet hands will allow you to push the pitch back off the silver).

After the pitch has hardened, apply the design to the back of the plate. Remember: *the design as you apply it will be in reverse when it is viewed from the other side.* Letters or numbers must be applied backwards.

The design is glued to the silver which is mounted in the pitch pot.

You can draw directly onto the silver. Use carbon paper and trace the design or, in the case of a repeat design, I make multiple copies and glue the design directly to the silver with rubber cement.

A stylus and a chasing hammer are used to transfer the design through the

The design after being transferred to the silver with stylus and hammer. About half of the repousse is complete.

paper onto the silver. Follow the entire design with a continuous series of hammered marks.

Remove the paper and you are ready to begin repoussing the design. The design is raised in general. Concentrate only on the more prominent sections of the design at this time.

If the silver begins to separate from the pitch, any more work will more than likely result in your piercing through or tearing the silver. When this happens the silver must be removed from the pitch by melting with a torch. Since the silver must be annealed anyway, the best way to remove the remaining pitch is to heat the silver to a cherry red. This will result in the pitch being reduced to a fine white ash.

A few steps should be taken before resetting in the pitch pot:

1. The silver should be cleaned with a good scale remover.

2. The silver should be straightened out to its original shape as much as possible.

3. The pitch pot must be prepared to accept the silver again. Chip out as much pitch as necessary. Add melted pitch in order to create a flat support surface.

The silver is reset and the repousse process continues. This process must be completed as many times as necessary, which will depend on your ability. (This project was reset in the pitch three times.)

Chasing

Repousse defines the design in general. During chasing the design takes on all the detail and character which you as an artist will be able to give it.

In the case of flowers and leaves, you must study nature, noticing the manner in which a leaf curls and how petals unfold. At this point, no amount of lecture or reading can replace the trial and error method of chasing.

The chasing side. Note the chased area as opposed to the unworked area.

Chasing is more delicate and much more laborious. At this point the design begins to come alive. For me, this is the fun part. It is where I am able to express myself as an artist. This is where I can communicate with someone, somewhere, at some time I know not when.

The chasing is about 90 percent completed.

After the final chasing has been completed, the piece is removed from the pitch, annealed and cleaned. A large steel block is used as a working surface. The chasing is again worked along the background, in order to straighten the edges and uniformly achieve the desired shape.

Buffing with bobbing compound will remove most of the small nicks and file marks. At this time stones are set if required and perhaps ball feet applied.

The completed project. It's mounted in the lid of an ebony box. Size: 9.5" x 7.5".

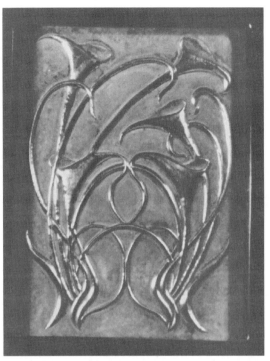

Is It For You?

Repousse and chasing as an art form is a demanding taskmaster and is not for everyone. Indeed, Ricardo's family tradition may very well end with him. But if you see art as I do, in terms of a bridge between what was, and what someday will be, you may discover repousse and chasing as enriching and rewarding as I have.

Art Nouveau Calla Littlies in an ebony box, repousse and chasing, brass and ebony, 9" x 7", 1991.

Spider Mum Plate, repousse and chasing, sterling silver, 3 ball feet, 7" dia., 1991.

I learned my craft of traditional silversmithing working with my friend and mentor, master craftsman, Richado Lopez De Grado. I learned the making of tools and hammers, planishing of metals, and the time consuming craft of repousse and chasing. This is a craft that goes back four thousand years. My five years of working with Ricardo has only given me an insight into the possibilities of what can be accomplished with this craft. I enjoy demonstrating to the public at craft shows, historical societies and museums. I feel it is my obligation to pass this knowledge on to future generations. This is a challenge I have set for myself, regardless of its outcome.

Marcia Lewis

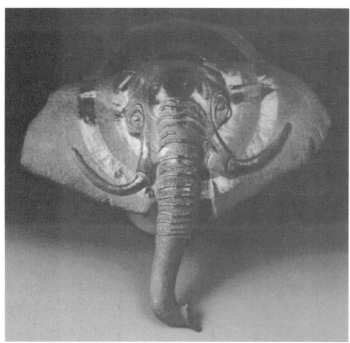

The Target Series V-5 Tusker, brooch, repousse and fabrication, silver and enamel, 3.5" x .25" x 3.5", 1989.

The Target Series V-2 Endangered Dolphin, brooch, repousse and fabrication, silver, 4.5" x .25" x 3", 1989.

Susan G. Neel-Goodsir

Bird, raised and bead blasted, copper, Plexiglas, brass, feathers and leather, 9" x 8" x 4", 1990.

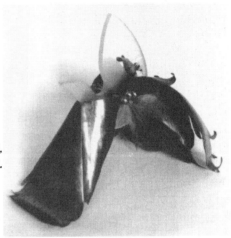

Bird, raised and bead blasted, copper, Plexiglas, brass, feathers and leather,9" x 8" x 4", 1990.

Bee, raised, cold connections, copper, brass, fur, leather and crystal, 12" x 9" x 5.75", 1992.

Bee, raised, cold connections, copper, brass, fur, leather and crystal, 12" x 9" x 5.75", 1992.

Bee, raised, cold connections, copper, brass, fur, leather and crystal, 12" x 9" x 5.75", 1992.

Photo credit: James R. Goodsir

Christina DePaul

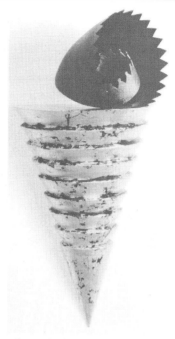

She Had A Lot On Her Mind, fabricated and lathe turned, anodized aluminum and wood, 9" x 4.5" x 37", 1990.*

The Gift, fabricated and lathe turned, anodized aluminum, wood and 24k gold leaf, 8" x 12" x 20", 1991.°

°Photo credit: Kevin Olds
*Photo credit: Bill Redic

He Could Wear Any Hat, fabricated, lathe turned and anodized, aluminum and wood, 9" x 4.5" x 33", 1991.°

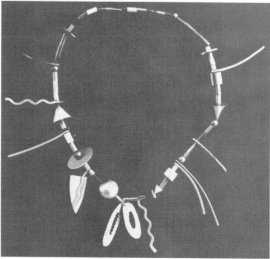

Untitled, fabricated and anodized, aluminum, 12" x 8" x 2", 1989.*

Sue Amendolara

Dancing Shakers, salt and pepper shakers, die formed, fabricated and carved, sterling silver, ebony, 24k gold foil and mother-of-pearl, 3" x 2" x 5": 4" x 1.5" x 4.5", 1991.°

Spiked Scent Bottle, fabricated, carved and keum-boo, sterling silver, ebony and 24k gold foil, 4" x 2" x 12", 1991.°

Venus Fly Trap Tea Infuser, formed and fabricated, hinge, sterling silver, 6" x 4" x 2", 1991.*

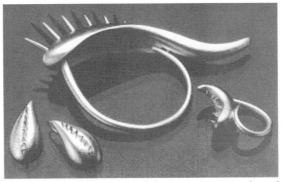

Barbed Jewelry, cast, fabricated, carved and keum-boo, sterling silver, ebony and 24k gold foil, 4" x 1.5" x 3.5", 1991.*

°Photo credit: Rick Potteiger
*Photo credit: Jeff Sabo

<u>Lynne Hull</u>

Basket #16, spun, copper and wood, 10" x 16" x 16", 1991.

Vertical Basket #10, spun, patinated copper, 14" x 7" x 7".

Basket #14, spun, patinated copper, 15" x 11" x 11", 1991.

Sharon K. Novak

Magic Vessel, fabricated, riveted, patinated and oxidized, brass and copper, 14" x 10" x 2", 1989.

Roger H. Horner

Untitled, spun, raised and fabricated, sterling, 5" x 5" x 6", 1990.

Untitled, spun, raised and fabricated, mokume and sterling, 4.5" x 3.5" x 8", 1990.

Merlin's Cup, spun, raised and fabricated, mokume and sterling, 4" x 4" x 6", 1990.

Untitled, spun and enameled, fine silver and enamel, 1.75" x 1.75" x 6", 1990.

Photo credit: Stanley Shockey

Cynthia Eid

Balance I, constructed, pewter, 3.5" x 2.5" x 8.5", 1990.

Peened Cups, raised, seamed and cross-peen hammer texture, sterling silver, 3" x 3" x 4", 1991.

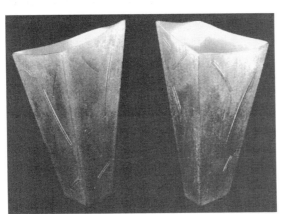

Arc Cups, inlay, scored and constructed, sterling silver and 14k gold, 4.25" x 2.25" x 2", 1991.

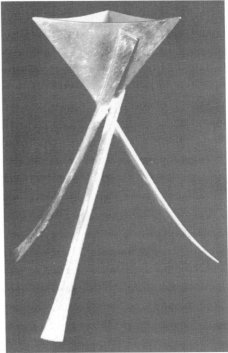

Goblet I, forged and constructed, brass and pewter, 5.5" x 5.5" x 7", 1990.

Joseph L. Brandom
Fredric B. DeVantier

Fredric B. DeVantier, Tulip, raised, fabricated and cast, sterling silver and 18k gold, 3" x 3" x 6.75", 1991. Photo credit: Robert Hirsch

Joseph L. Brandom, Vessel, raised and fabricated, pewter, 18" x 10", 1991. Photo credit and copyright 1991 Lance Morgan

Tracy Gawley
Jeff Georgantes

Jeff Georgantes, Vessel, cast, green patina, bronze, 8" x 8" x 10", 1991.

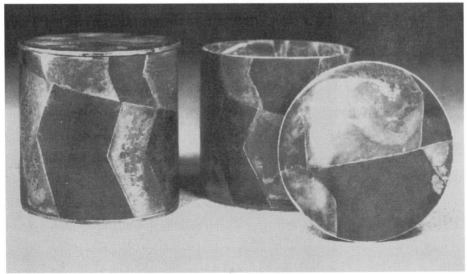

Tracy Gawley, Married Metal Boxes, married metals, copper and bronze, 2" x 1", 1991. Photo credit: Charles Lewton-Brain

Elizabeth Gilbert
Humphrey Gilbert

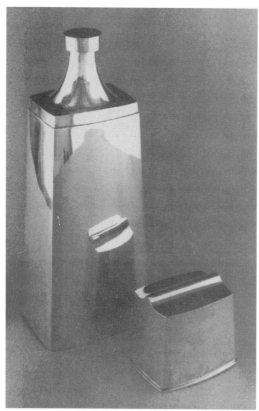

Humphrey Gilbert, Decanter, fabricated and raised, sterling silver, 3" x 4" x 11", 1989.

Photo credit: Rory O'Neill

Elizabeth Gilbert, Arrow Earrings, fabricated and forged, sterling, jasper and black onyx, 3", 1992.

John Edwards
Linda Weiss Edwards

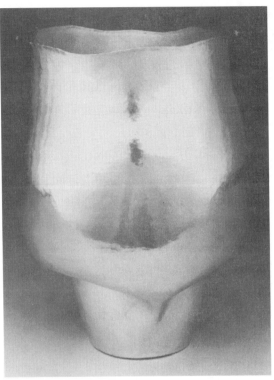

Linda Weiss Edwards, Vessel #130 - Jardiniere, raised, sterling silver, 6" x 7" x 9", 1990. Photo credit: George Post. Copyright 1990 Linda Weiss Edwards

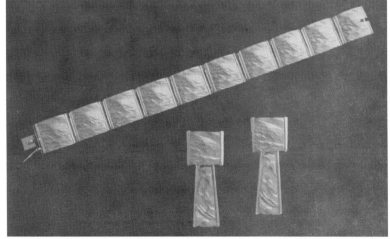

John and Linda Edwards, Untitled, bracelet and earring set, cast and fabricated, 18k gold, B: 7.5", 1990. Photo credit: John Edwards and George Post. Copyright 1990 Linda Weiss Edwards

Modes of Working

by Charles Lewton-Brain

When considering the current stirrings towards more and better documentation in the contemporary metals world, I would like to share some thoughts on the ways that you and I might choose to work and compose as jewelers.

Blue/Rod/Birds, anodized aluminum and electroformed copper, aluminum, gold plate, copper, steel and paint, ea: 4"L, 1991.

I think it is useful to analyze systems and give names to their parts so as to be able to discuss them. Therefore we will look at some of the ways that people approach working in the field; their modes of working. I've rather arbitrarily decided to call them *industry, fashion, process oriented, formal, intuitive, expressionist, folk, conceptual, political and confrontational, international,* and *jewellery as image.* By considering such categories' one can choose or at least observe how one works and with which biases. More conscious decision making allows greater choice and freedom in composition. Some people concentrate within a given mode while others, such as Barbara Heinrich, work across the entire spectrum of choices. Like most, I use many aspects when I work. The following are brief definitions of these working modes.

Industry

This is the cast gold and gem work one sees in most commercial jewelry stores. Design variations are often limited and conventions such as the use of white gold heads with yellow shanks and standard gold alloys are common. In jewellery, just as in Detroit car design, older designs are disassembled into components and re-arranged according to commercial conventions. This jewellery almost always uses precious metals with gemstones. The importance and value of the work is as *product*. The context and references of the work are commercial, social, economic and status. Work is also produced that functions as a type of signifier, a uniform telling the viewer about the achievements, religious, organizational, corporate or economic affiliations of the wearer.

Fashion

This jewelry resembles that seen in fashion magazines. It is mass produced. It also sells well for a time, then is superseded by a different or varied mass produced style. Marketing is an integral part of what makes fashion jewellery sell. Marketing occurs using images.

Fashion jewellery is frequently made of inexpensive materials. The design or surfaces are often derived from some element of International or Art oriented modes of working. The design strength is often watered down from the original type. The quality of the work is usually compromised by market factors, aspects of function and manufacturing and production requirements. Nevertheless this jewellery serves as a useful conduit by which ideas pass from a relatively small avante garde group of innovators to the general public, creating a slow change in what constitutes acceptable design to the buying public.

Process oriented

The final resolution of this jewellery is influenced or guided by the working process. The artist is open to serendipity and utilizing effects produced by the process. The marks of process are used as part of

Concrete Coffee Pot, cement, wood, urethane foam, sterling silver, steel and paint, 14" x 10" x 4", 1992.

the compositional design. Visual feedback is used to determine the composition of the object. Decisions are made in an aesthetic response to changes observed during the making. The form is derived from the working process plus the nature of the material, rather than being forced on it, as may happen in other modes of working.

Formal

The composition consists of fixed or regular elements organized according to traditional or non-traditional design rules: strict design. Often the elements are simple in form, sometimes geometric. The organization is based on rhythms, visual balance and mass, texture, color, and form relationships. While the jewellery may make references to other works, it is in a formal manner and is essentially self-sufficient; able to stand by itself without knowledge of context or reference. (To some extent, all working modes involve some kind of formal approach to composition.)

Intuitive

Work that is made in ignorance of, or deletion of, traditional or accepted design rules. The maker decides during the working process what "feels right" rather than being governed by formal compositional rules and systems. This can result from active avoidance or the discarding of design rules. Instead, this often results from educational institutions that no longer teach 2D and 3D design. This has become, to my mind, the all too common practice in North America this last decade or so. I would not wish everyone to follow rigid rules of extreme formalism. If students have an understanding of design then they can refer to or dispose of it at will. Intuitive work is by no means naive. An experienced practitioner will have developed their own system of personal design rules and considerations, symbols and repeated relationships of elements, colors, textures and references, all of which are manipulated in a formal manner that is personal to the maker.

Glasses 6, steel, brass, paint, silicon carbide and lenses, 1989. Model: Dee Fontans

Expressionistic

Work that deals with emotions; emotive expression. When such work appears in jewellery there is often a relationship to recent events in painting. It usually involves a less geometric approach to design and often uses imagery. Sometimes narrative, it refers to personal feelings. Personal symbols are created. Elements and materials are assigned symbolic value and their meaning and relationships to other symbols and elements in the work become a compositional element. Some people work intuitively, others more formally. Bruce Metcalfe's work, for example, deals with expressionist issues. Such work is often artist-centered, that is, it serves as a way for the artist to externalize their psychological concerns. It is then less audience dependent and interactive, though part of its role may be evoking emotions. We can see and infer information from the work, its materials and symbols. Even so, part of it is private, available only when the artist chooses to reveal it to us. The expressionistic mode creates a mystery.

Folk

This jewellery is made according to the established tradition of an ethnic or culturally defined group. Western commercial jewellery is almost a type of "folk" jewellery. because of its numerous conventions.

Conceptual

This type of jewellery is related to *international*, *political* and *confrontational* work. The idea is of paramount importance; the piece exists to service the idea. It provokes thought and questioning. Often a juxtaposition of elements or contexts is used. Formal composition, material and subject each service the concept. While the piece may stand on its own, the provoked thought is necessary for full understanding. Sometimes a piece is made for the small, insular jewellery world and that context is necessary to understand the work as it is played (in a theatrical sense) for other jewellers. Otto Kunzli and Peter Skubic are examples in this genre. It seems to me that the market, salability and preciousness as an issue prevent many North Americans from approaching jewellery in this manner.

Political and Confrontational

Political jewellery derives from or refers to political issues, usually current ones. Humor, irony and satire may often appear in political work. Confrontational jewelry is designed to provoke a reaction or response in the viewer. The response desired may be pro or con to the subject addressed or it may simply be to raise questions in the viewers mind. For its function to be fulfilled, it must be interactive with the viewer. This is special in that it uses the viewers experience and thought to complete itself, a quality it shares with conceptual work. The roles and contexts of propaganda are often important in dealing with such work. Examples of it might include campaign buttons and the work of Harriet Estel Berman.

International

This is the "New Jewelry" of Ralph Turner and Peter Dormer. I might define it as jewelry that resembles in style the work published in the international magazines and major exhibition catalogs in any period of several years. It is a phenomenon of image, that is, that it exists and is experienced and responded to internationally primarily as image and media product.

Jewellery As Image

I inferred above that "New Jewelry" is dependent on and effects responses in working goldsmiths by means of magazines, catalogs and other images: documentation. Its influence is worldwide and real, but the work is experienced as photographic images by most people interacting with it. The physical experience of the work is removed -- and so are subtleties of visual and tactile experience that normally provide much information about an object. Peter Dormer writing in the December 1987 Lemel (Australia) notes that "New Jewelry" is often disappointing when viewed in person. Nevertheless, communication through imagery is a vital, real method of interaction between makers. Those who experiment with light projections as jewelry or set up careful photographs have recognized the nature of what they are doing and understand that their creation is not physical jewellery, but a *reference to* it. It is essential to make images of your work and share them with others. Just don't confuse an image object and experience with an physical object and expedience.

To conclude, the foregoing definitions may be useful as a way of evaluating how one works or likes to work and therefore allow one greater choice in how to work, design and compose.

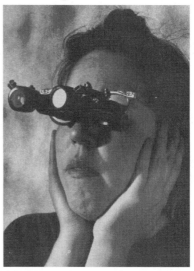

Glasses 2, lenses, plastic, glass, steel, brass and paint, 1989. Model: Dee Fontans

Charles Lewton-Brain studied and worked in Europe and North America. He lectures and publishes internationally on his research in rapid methods of manipulating metal and it's surface for artistic and manufacturing purposes. He teaches at the Alberta College of Art (since 1986) and writes, exhibits and works in his studio. He thinks of himself as an artist who works primarily in the context of body ornament.

Nancy Worden

If I Only Had A Brain, fabricated, silver, saphires, pearl, rutilated quartz, glass, straw and paper, 2" x .5" x 2", 1991.

Motivation, fabricated, silver, glass, copper, paper, garnet and malachite, 19.5" x .5" x 2", 1992.

Goodbye Old Paint, fabricated, silver, plastic, glass, photo and rubies, 2.5" x .75" x 2", 1992.

Home Repairs, fabricated, silver, steel, glass, paper, citrine and sawdust, 2" x .5" x 1.5", 1991.

Photo credit: Lynn Hamrick

Dee Fontans

Miles in the Arctic, fabric and dingle balls, 1992.

Untitled, fabric and plastic, 18" x 8", 1992.

Earth Balls, compressed aluminum foil, epoxy resin and gold leaf, 1992.

Untitled, fabric and dingle balls, 1992.

Photo credit: Charles Lewton-Brain

Vittoria Cozzi-Olivetti

S. Passle Hordinski

Vittoria Cozzi-Olivetti, Esther, fabricated, forged and woven, sterling silver, German silver, Nugold, brass, pearls and antique silk, 1989. Photo credit: Tomaso Bradshaw

S. Passle Hordinski, Breast Plate, tubular knitting, sterling silver, rayon and paper core, 36" x 30" x 36", 1992. Photo credit: Greg Helminski

Wings Neckpiece, weaving, sterling silver and nylon, 15" x 12", 1990.

Flora Book

Collar, weaving, Mizuhiki (paper cord), 14" x 11", 1990.

Willow Neckpiece, weaving, sterling silver and nylon, 16" x 10", 1990.

Photo credit: Roger Schreiber

Sharon Hall

*Neckpiece #5: Lighter Than Air Series, cut pieces laced together, ribbon,
Polycarbonate and permanent marker, 26" dia x flat, 1991.*

*Neckpiece #5: Lighter Than Air Series, cut pieces laced together, ribbon,
Polycarbonate and permanent marker, 26" dia x flat, 1991.*

Jewelry Marks / Maker's Marks

by Daloma Armentrout

Jewelry marks have long served to identify makers and guarantee quality or authenticity. Today, registered trademarks and copyright notice inform us about various rights and responsibilities we bear each other in the artistic and commercial aspects of creation and exchange. One benefit of using jewelry marking consistent with current regulations is that your original work will receive greater respect. Also, those who infringe on your rights may be prosecuted. Another benefit is that your mark can be used as a marketing tool, to strengthen your "designer original" image. A third boon is to the future of jewelry scholarship and research; those of us who follow paper trails need greater documen-

tation. In fact, much of metalsmithing history and appraisal research is constructed from a comparative study of jewelry marks. Perhaps some of that history will illuminate current Art Jewelry issues.

Hallmarks

Hallmarking, as generally used, refers to the practice of stamping a code or symbol on an article made of precious metal, to indicate the quality (fineness) and quality standards used. Hallmarks were originally the "mark of the hall" of medieval production or craft guilds entrusted with setting quality standards and testing products for compliance. Guilds and trade associations regulating quality included professions from baker (weight and quality standards) to goldsmith. Precious metal content has been regulated by governmental decree in both France (Montpellier and other townmarks) and England (Goldsmith's Hall, London) since c. 1200-1300. "Hallmark" has become, somewhat inaccurately, a generic term,

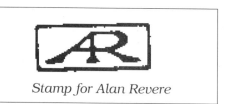
Stamp and registered trademark for Charles Lewton-Brain.

used to include many different types of marks: maker's marks, trademarks and quality marks. British and other European hallmarks are legally defined, and differ from each other and from those of the US; for this reason, the term "hallmark" is used here in a limited sense.

British and European Hallmarks

As the historic basis for practice in this country, it may be helpful to examine the compulsory British Hallmarks. These comprise the "Maker's Mark," the British-made "Standard Mark," the "Assay Office Mark" and the "Date Letter." The Maker's Mark has been required since the 14th century, and since 1720 has been a monogram composed of the maker's first- and last-name initials. The British-made Standard Mark for gold is first a crown, then numbers in a hexagonal shield indicating fineness (since 1932: 375, 585, 750, 916). For sterling silver (925 fineness), the Standard Mark is a lion passant (in use since 1544), for Brittania silver (950), Brittania seated (since 1697); for platinum, a cross-surmounted orb in a pentagonal shield. The Assay Office Mark, traditionally London (leopard's head), may alternatively be Birmingham (anchor), Edinburgh (castle) or Sheffield (rose). Date letters be-

gan in the 15th century; these stamps are employed, then destroyed, annually.

Other European countries use similar patterns and traditions of marking; however, specific marks and requirements for marking do vary. An international convention for the acceptance of quality control stamps, and for the maintenance of standards through assay, has been signed by many European countries.

United States

While such an historically elaborate and detailed use of marks is not required in the United States, many marking regulations and patterns have emerged. The Jewelers' Vigilance Committee has recommended to the Federal Trade Commission the acceptance of the *Guides for the Jewelry Industry;* the Guide addresses marking, among other ethical trade practices. These guidelines were established to combat deceptive trade practices, such as underkarating and misrepresentation. Most of the recommendations are quite sound for most of the jewelry industry. The practices of marking employed by craftspeople and artists, however, sometimes vary from this prescription.

This is rarely in an attempt to deceive; more often, studio or metalsmithing traditions have taken precedence over those of the commercial jewelry industry. Many technical and material combinations used by artists do not lend themselves well to industrial-strength marking. Proper limitations for such marks as "handmade," for instance, are debatable. The *Guides for the Jewelry Industry* regulate all attachments,

Stamp for Alan Revere

tags, invoices, etc. as though they constituted quality marking; therefore, it may be prudent for the designer-artist to identify both materials and quality with great care. Descriptions provided to the retail gallery, as well as on counter cards or attached "authenticity" cards, require accuracy before prose. Of the many marks which may be found on an artist/goldsmith article produced in the US, perhaps the most common are the "Quality Mark" and "Maker's Mark."

Quality Marks may be content number — as in European marking — or the more common US 1/24 gold karatage marks: 10k, 14k, 18k, 22k. Silver may be stamped "sterling," or the piece may be inscribed "Ag 925"; other fineness marks include "coin" (900) and "fine silver." Platinum group metals may be marked. Special alloys and patination/alloy techniques may be noted. Contemporary designer and art jewelry may be marked to indicate any combination of the precious, non-ferrous, ferrous and refractory metals; other materials usually are not noted in marks.

Maker's Marks may be the signature or logo of the designer, the benchmark of the specific artist, a registered trademark or a combination of these. A special case is the

Stamp for the Noble Metal Company, Joann Pedersen Lutz

workshop or atelier mark, as distinguished from the individual designer-maker's mark or signature; this parallels the use of a design firm mark, along with the benchmark of the actual maker. Honorary society marks, a sort of "aesthetic value hall-

mark," are found in a few cases; the Society of North American Goldsmiths (SNAG) Distinguished Member stamp is just such a designation.

Distinguished Member stamp for the Society of North American Goldsmiths

Copyright notice often is encountered when examining designer or art jewelry today; patent notice may infrequently be found. In art jewelry and objects, "Titles" and "Series Marks" may appear, as may inscribed text or other surface marks unique to the work. In an artist-created work, a signature and date may be found, sometimes in addition to other markings. However, such marks alone cannot prove the authenticity, origin or actual maker of the work; inconsistent marking is common, and fraudulent marks are known.

US Trademarks

Trademarks may have origins in the pictographic symbols placed on ancient goods and tallies to indicate their source and ownership. This practice assisted in trade, accounting and recovery. Today, the "Registered Trademark" (design or logo, monogram, numbers or names) serves to identify the manufacturer and thus to guarantee product reliability. In this sense, the US trademark on jewelry combines the functions of the British Maker's Mark and Assay Office Mark. Although historic US silver- and goldsmiths occasionally marked their creations, no outside regulation of metals quality and standards was in place. The 1906 Federal Stamping Law and subsequent amendments (usually referred to collectively as the National Stamping Act) emplaced commercial standards and stamping regulations. For interstate commerce, goods bearing Quality Marks must be within certain standard deviations (tolerances) of fineness, solder included. Additionally, a Quality Mark may not be used unless a Trademark is placed in conjunction with it; further, the Trademark must be registered ® with the US Department of Commerce Patent and Trademark Office, or application for registration must be filed.

These regulations, like most, have been formulated under the advice of ethical tradespeople acting to serve the best interests of the client, and to enhance their own

Stamps for Claire Pfleger

commitment to fair practices. In fact, prime proponents of quality standards and trademarking include the Jewelers Vigilance Committee and The Jewelers' Circular Keystone. JC-K publishes the *Brand Name and Trademark Guide* (11th ed. currently available), a key resource for researching current Maker's Marks. Marks in this publication are organized in categories (monograms, designs without letters, company names, and numbers) and are indexed by company name and address. The 12th edition is to be published this year, and will include more contemporary designer and artist marks. Some of these marks were collected and submitted by this author and have not yet been registered. Trademark claim, TM, may be used without application for registration, to indicate a claim of ownership; such use may strengthen other forms of protection, such as copyright claims.

While the requirements of the National Stamping Act have benefits (especially to the researching appraiser or historian), they are by no means universally followed. First, no federal regulation requires Quality Marks; but *if* quality is represented, and *if* the item is to be transported beyond state lines, then it must conform to the federal requirements regarding tolerances and trademarking. (Some states also have regulations concerning trademarks and trade names). The article should be marked before sold. Some manufacturers produce articles without marks; the distributor or vendor then becomes the marker, and bears the responsibility for Quality Marks in association with their Trademark. This occurs at all levels of the market. One instance of this is a production house providing finished pieces, often of superior quality, to a name jeweler or design firm. The marks will reflect the design firm or retailer, rather than the actual production manufacturer. Fraudulent trademarks are encountered. Well-known design houses sometimes publicize the manner in which they mark authentic editions for certain years (e.g.: in a lozenge, upside down or on a certain part of the article). Registered trademark holders may pursue action against counterfeiters, for both civil and criminal penalties. Trademark infringement cases in federal court may result in recovery of profits, damages and costs, attorneys fees, and, possible treble damages.

US Copyrights ©
Copyrights generally operate to identify the owner of the rights of reproduction: copying. The nature of copyright is that interwoven interests are served by this constitutionally-mandated, statutory grant of rights: the creative, the commercial, and the promotion of learning or access for

the public good. The creation of new works is encouraged by the incentive of reproduction protections; the creator is granted copyright for a limited time. Entrepreneurial needs are met by instituting a method for the exchange of an economically valuable right; copyrights may be assigned so that works may be commercially produced. The public good is served by new works becoming broadly available for use, and eventually entering the public domain.

More and more frequently, "Copyright Notice" is marked on jewelry and associated articles, and on the visual images used in promoting them (ads, brochures, catalogs, etc.). Notice is accomplished by stamping or inscribing the word "Copyright," "Copr," or the symbol ©, the copyright holder's name, and the year (which may be omitted in jewelry). Copyright law allows an "alternate designation" for name on jewelry; trade practice is to use the Trademark. (While the present law recognizes only marks consisting of letters and numbers, as opposed to designs or logos, this inconsistent application is expected to be revised.)

An article is awarded copyright for original artistic or aesthetic creation in its form, and is protected in its particulars. Functional, mechanical or utilitarian aspects are not protected. For instance, the belt buckle is not copyrightable. However, a particular form or design on the belt buckle may receive copyright protections. The amount of originality and creativity involved in a copyrightable work may be minimal; the amount of alteration of the form's particulars allowed while still retaining claim protection is usually held to be about 10%.

[Editor's note: 10% is NOT written into the copyright law and cannot be counted on as a legal amount of alteration, even though it is generally accepted outside of a court of law.]

Stamp for Mark Knipe

Limited copyright protections ("bare rights") exist by virtue of the mere creation of a copyrightable work of artistic craftsmanship or intellectual property. Copyrights are perfected through the process of registration and notice. While it is not safe to assume that articles which do not give notice may be freely copied, copyright infringement cases are most successful when engaged pursuant to prior registration and notice. Notice may be strengthened when achieved by use of a monogram or signature registered as a trademark; notice alone allows 60 days copyright protection. The length of perfected copyright protection is now the life of the artist, plus 50 years; registered works created prior to 1978 require copyright renewal. Pre-1978 works which were distributed without notice may have irrevocably lost copyright protection, entering the public domain. Claims of copyright infringement may result in actual or statutory damages, with attorney's fees. Copyright claims may be registered with the Library of Congress Copyright Office.

Tangible Property/ Intangible Rights

In the US, constitutional protections for private property have been expanded through federal and local legislation. Intellectual property can be seen as part of the tangible object; intellectual property rights attend the property. Rights may be assigned or conveyed. Infringement of rights is a form of theft, and damages may be awarded. Producer, designer and artist's rights may be protected, controlled and enforced under various federal and state statutes. Registered Trademarks and Copyrights serve to notify the public of certain rights and responsibilities borne by the manufacturer or designer, many of which have monetary value in and of themselves. For instance, the right to produce or distribute an article with a trademark or brand name may be sold, licensed or leased. The right to reproduce an original work is not conveyed with sale of the article, with the publication of its image, or by virtue of its "use" (being worn). This right is reserved to the copyright holder, who may choose whether or not to convey permission for reproduction of the work, and at what price. Patent protections offer the opportunity to file injunctions against and seek damages from all infringers — including ultimate distributors. "Design Patents," available for unique (rather than simply original) designs, are most commonly found at a fairly high level of commercial design and production. "Trade dress" infringement cases have become a method for protection and redress of design rights; trade dress protects unique style and presentation. And many of the concepts of intellectual property protection have been addressed internationally by the Berne Convention for the Protection of Literary and Artistic Works.

Maker's Mark for Jan Yager

Art Jewelry Issues:
Double Jeopardy

Why do we -- appraisers, historians, creative jewelers, gallery directors and artists — need to know about various rights and responsibilities, and what has this to do with art jewelry? Jewelry collectors and clients seek professional opinions from independent appraisers, who rely on scholarly and market research. Galleries are liable to their clients for the information they provide; metalsmiths are liable to their galleries; gemstone and metals dealers to metalsmiths. We each have rights, and with rights come responsibilities.

We know that trademarks help identify the designer or manufacturer, "guarantee" quality, establish provenance, and add to value. Trademarks may indicate select sources for conducting research, or for acquiring articles for resale. But consider also the effects of after-market alterations or repairs on the *authentication* of a trademarked watch, vessel or jewelry article. The trademarker may disclaim the article, because it has been altered beyond their standards. This affects its authenticity for valuation purposes and for further marketing. We bear *the makers* a responsibility not to alter their works, and then represent them as authentic. Additionally, makers or manufacturers bear a responsibility to identify materials, quality and edition accurately when using their mark or signature.

Consider the propriety of cost-analysis appraisal for replacement value of an original jewel. This is a common practice, albeit an indefensible approach to valuation of art collectibles. How can an appraiser properly assess a value of "reproduction cost" when the *right to reproduce* is restricted legally and economically via copyright protections? No other manufacturer may have that right. How can one even know the art jeweler's "cost"? Market research is the appropriate appraisal approach, but appraisers usually can't find the right markets unless jewelry markings lead them there. Appraisers and manufacturers bear a responsibility to respect original works. Makers need to represent works as such by providing copyright notice and/

Stamps for Alexandra Solowij Watkins,
Atelier Janiyé Inc.

or maker's registered trademarks.

Courts have held that the *fact of copying* can satisfy requirements for trade dress protections. Some of these same rights/ responsibilities and concepts were invoked by the Berne Convention, to which the US is a signatory. International rights, protections and markings are exceedingly complex, and greatly affect legal import/export practices. At the same time, our fine designer jewelry markets and art jewelry collections are becoming very much an international affair.

Now, add to the above concerns those issues involved in the federal Visual Artists Rights Act of 1990. These statutes hold that rights in original work may extend to the right of attribution, the right to disclaim altered works, and even some rights of conservation of the work. Care to suggest refashioning or melting down an original work of artist made jewelry, without reference to the artist's potential rights and redress? Presently, several states are considering legislation which endows artists with continuing economic rights in their work, providing for future compensation (like royalties) at each level of exchange. Our rights and responsibilities are being expanded.

The very nature of collectible articles is such that the marks (trademark, signature, title, series) alone may contribute a great deal to our understanding of the

work -- and to the value assigned by collectors, appraisers and academics. Yet marking patterns are inconsistent. There is not yet one standard practice for actual artist-created, limited editions. Unique works (one-off) with signature and title will be critically assessed and economically valued differently than a numbered limited edition series so marked. Actual limited editions are evaluated differently than open-ended studio "production-by demand." And short studio production runs are very different from "in stock" industrial mass-manufacturing. Perhaps we need to investigate the marking conventions of other artforms, such as limited edition lithographs, to evolve a better standard practice regarding edition marking.

Conclusion

Journals and other periodicals in the fields of metalsmithing, fine craft and design scholarship are encouraged to publish drawings or photographs of Maker's Marks or signatures alongside articles or photo-portfolios featuring artist made jewelry and metals. Why not place your mark by each photograph in this publication?

[Editor's note: a published signature may be used against you by a forger.]

Designer jewelers are urged to use their logo or other trademark in promotional material, for better overall name-product recognition. Counter cards, biographies, advertisements, artist's statements and

Stamp for Harriete Estel Berman

even tags or invoices can carry your mark. Why not provide your galleries with a name and mark display card? This type of recognition can assist in securing trade-dress protections, as well.

An effort to collect Maker's Marks, and to record patterns in marking has begun. Each and every reader is invited to contribute to this effort, by recording the marks, types of articles produced, and contact information for designers and artists encountered in their practice. The author has found photographs, line drawings, stamp impressions and slides all to be useful resources; these will be gratefully accepted for inclusion in her registry of marks.

It is hoped that such attention to detail will not only support better appraisal research and reporting in the present, but will be of benefit to artists, collectors, historians, critics and academics pursuing research in the future. Otherwise, it may be "game over" for the jewelry artist when we've only just begun.

Stamp fo Nancy Michel, Atelier Janiyé Inc.

Bibliography:
American Jewelry Manufacturers, Dorothy Rainwater, 1988, Schiffer Pub Ltd.

Art Jewelry & Metals, Markets, Meaning, Daloma Armentrout, 1992, Armentrout-Hawken Appraisal Assoc.

The Crafts Report, "Stop Thief! Craftspeople Fight Knockoffs,"Judith Mitchell,March 1992.

--"Beware of Imitation, Influence and Theft," Milton Townsend, March 1991.

--"Protecting Your Name is Good Business," Leonard DuBoff, Oct 1991.

--"Take a Few Basic Steps to Copyright Your Work," Leonard DuBoff, May 1991.

--"Limited Editions: How Many is Too Many?" Leonard DuBoff, May 1991.

JC-K Brand Name and Trademark Guide, 11th ed. 1984, *Jewelers' Circular/ Keystone.*

Jewelry Concepts and Technology, Oppi Untracht, 1982, Doubleday & Co, Inc.

Recommendations to Revise the Federal Trade Commission "Guides for the Jewelry Industry," Jewelers Vigilance Committee, 1986.

Stamp for Miyé Matsukata, Atelier Janiyé Inc.

For further information contact:
The Commissioner of Patents & Trademarks, Patent & Trademark Office, US Department of Commerce, Washington DC 20231.

Information & Publications Section, LM-455, Copyright Office, Library of Congress, Washington, DC 20559.

Daloma Armentrout, Designated Member of the International Society of Appraisers, is a consultant in art metals and jewelry design research, marketing and education. With her partner, gemologist Anne Hawken, she practices in Austin, Santa Fe and throughout the southwest. Her new publication Art Jewelry & Metals: *Makers, Markets, Meaning* is available from Armentrout-Hawken Associates, 6034 W. Courtyard Dr, Suite 305, Austin, TX 78730.

Ben Dyer

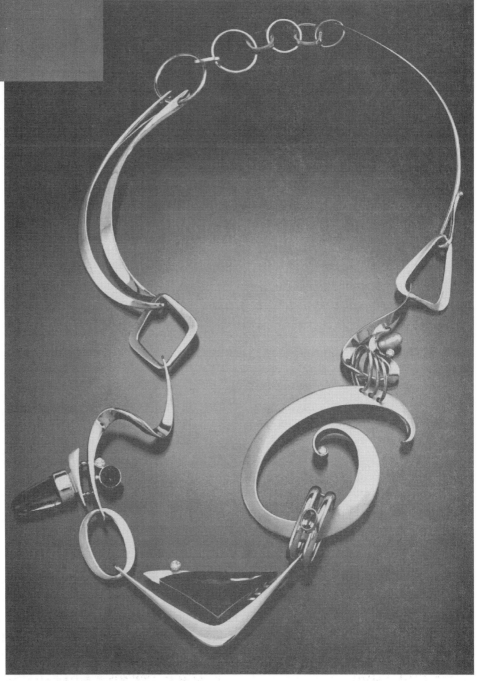

Crest of the Wave, brooch, fabricated and forged, 14k, lapis, diamonds and pearls. Photo credit: Ralph Gabriner

Mother's Playful Illusion, 14k, diamonds, tourmalines, pink pearl and psilomoline, 1991. Copyright 1991 Ben Dyer

Adam Alexander Shirley

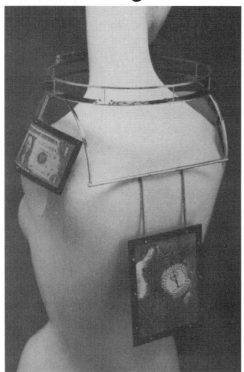

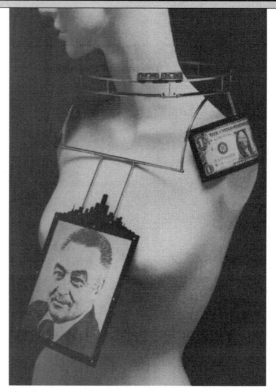

God Save Our City, Mayor Coleman Young Neckpiece, cast, fabricated, screen printed, riveted and hinged, sterling silver and aluminum, 22" x 18" x 4.5", 1992.

God Save Our City, Mayor Coleman Young Neckpiece, cast, fabricated, screen printed, riveted and hinged, sterling silver and aluminum, 22" x 18" x 4.5", 1992.

*Photo credit: Tim Thayer

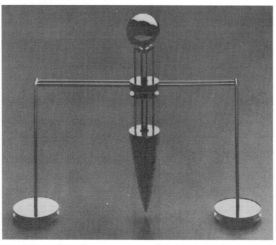

Vertex Infundere, cast and fabricated, sterling silver, gold and steel spring, 1.25" x 1.25" x 5", 1991.*

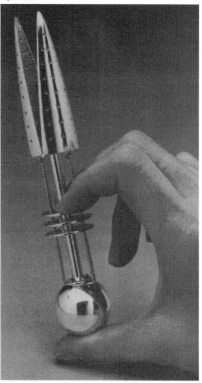

Vertex Infundere, cast and fabricated, sterling silver, gold and steel spring, 1.25" x 1.25" x 5", 1991.*

Diane Marshall

Buying the American Dream, pendant, fabricated, stamped and riveted, sterling silver, brass, amber glass lens and a b/w photo, 2" x 2", 1992.

My Life In Flames, pin, fabricated, nickel silver, sterling, wire and matchsticks, 1.5" x 1.5", 1990.

Carpe Diem, earrings, formed and stamped, copper, nickle, aluminum and sterling, 1" x 2", 1991.

Photo credit: Sara Jorde

Nicole Jacquard

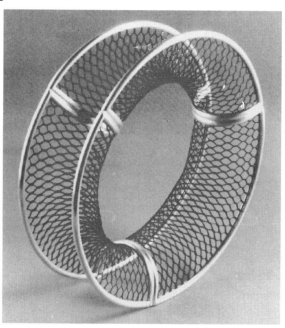

Neck Collar, anodized, sterling silver and aluminum, 8" x 2.5", 1992.

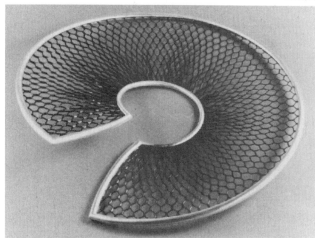

Bracelet, anodized, sterling silver and aluminum, 8" x 2.5" x 8", 1992.

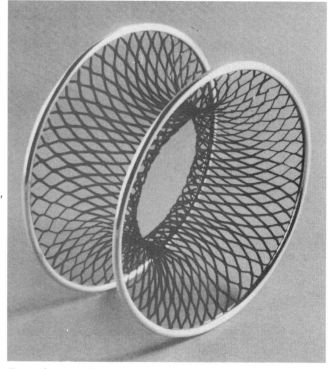

Photo credit: Elizabeth Barick Fall and Melissa Muszynski

Bracelet, anodized, sterling silver and aluminum, 4.5" x 4.5" x 2.5", 1992.

Mask II, forged, folded form and coiled basketry, oxidized copper and pine needles, 5" x 5" x 2.5", 1991. (Mask is the lid.)

Crys Harse

Victoria, braided with coiled basketry, sterling silver, lace agate and pine needles, 4.5" x 2.5" x 5", 1991.

The Eye Within, forged, set stone and coiled basketry, oxidized copper, tiger eye and pine needles, 4" x 4" x 2.5", 1989. Photo credit: Charles Lewton-Brain

Pagoda, fold formed and coiled basketry, copper, red oxide patina and pine needles, 5" x 5" x 4", 1990. Photo credit: John Dean

Watsonian Approaches

by Lynda Watson-Abbott

When David asked me to contribute to the 1992 survey by writing about my current work, I was hesitant. Since this is specifically a jewelry/metals book, I wasn't sure that it was appropriate. Metal is still an important part of my pieces although I am no longer making jewelry. My motivation, intent and ideas haven't changed, they have evolved.

Looking back on more than 25 years of metalwork (and drawings from many years before that), I understand that my work, regardless of media, has always served the same purpose and come from the same place. It records everything. My work serves as a journal of my life, travels, attitudes, experiences and relationships. Over the years, "places" have become the tangible symbols that I use. As my pieces have evolved, they are more and more literal. The recent (1987-90) architectural and structural brooches represent my attitudes about exercise and time constraints, practical and ecological concerns, friendships,

events and many other things. They are small, simple and abbreviated. Although these pieces are packed with *personal* information, I realize that probably no one

¿Como? Imodium, roll printed and carved, Prismacolor pencil on paper, wood, nickle silver and tacks, 15" x 9.75" x 1.25", 1991*.

116

who observes them has an inkling as to their reason for being. I have never really cared too much -- rarely attempted too explain or elaborate -- feeling that I had satisfied my needs, sort of...

Lately these metal pieces have begun to make me uncomfortable. Working with metal is very satisfying, but it is a time and labor intensive material and the wearable jewelry format has limitations. I have had a creeping urge to be more explicit or complete; to allow the imagery to explain itself. I wish to evoke a response or possibly share an understanding or tell a story. I want to expand my options, and do the kind of explaining that can be done best (by me) with pens, pencils and paints -- in addition to metal.

Until I was a senior in college (when I took my first metals class) my art experience had been primarily with graphic media. I have suffered from lack of "graphic inclusion" in my "real work" for a long time

*¿Como? Pepto Bismol, roll printed and tooled copper, patinated, Prismacolor pencils on paper, wood and copper, 16" x 12.75" x 1.25", 1991.**

*¿Como? Raidolitos, roll printed, hydralic pressed and patinated, Prismacolor pencils on paper, wood and copper. 14" x 8.75" x 1.25", 1991.**

*Photo credit: V. Vaughn Visnius

but have never found a satisfactory way to combine (both) disciplines.

While spending most of the summer of 1991 in Mexico, my direction became clear. We were all amused and frustrated by our inability to communicate (especially the simplest things) even when we had practiced both verbiage and delivery. The response was most frequently "¿Como?" accompanied by a sincerely confused look. At the same time, we were becoming intimately familiar with a whole group of "things" and products that we don't use, eat, ride, do or deal with at home. They were incorporated into our lives and our queries regarding them often elicited the "¿Comos?" It became a visual game for me. I began substituting the "things" for (appropriate) items in the house or environs. The more I thought about these "pieces" and played with the images, the more they evolved into tangible forms -- drawings with metal frames that completed or enhanced the imagery. The *COMO* drawings are done with Prismacolor pencils. The frames are made of wood wrapped or otherwise embellished with metal which has been textured, printed, pressed, tooled and colored to complete, intensify or explain the drawings. The interaction is one that I have been seeking for sometime and the possibilities are exciting. *This work is more enjoyable than anything I've done recently.*

Ideas for new pieces using the same format abound. A new series of pencil drawings about "night lights" is in the process and different metals are being explored for frames. The learning process continues.

Regardless of where this work goes, I am who I am. I have a great affinity for and loyalty to metal as a medium, metals education and especially the metals community. I assume that I will always think of myself as a metalsmith. However, truth be told, I am not as much a metalsmith as a chronicler of my own ideas and experiences. I think that what is important is that we understand our motivations in terms of content and not in terms of medium or process. It seems to me that being a metalsmith or jeweler is great as long as the content needs are satisfied, but one should never hesitate to move to another material or discipline if ideas can be better realized in it. Besides, the more one learns about materials and processes, the larger the vocabulary available for use -- whatever the motivation.

For the last 22 years I have taught the jewelry/metals program at Cabrillo College in Santa Cruz County, CA.

I received both my MA and MFA in jewelry/metalsmithing at Cal State University, Long Beach.

¿Como? Amarilla Flecha, sawing, filing and drilling, Prismacolor pencils on paper, wood, brass and paint, 16.5" x 15.75" x 1.25", 1991. Photo credit: V. Vaughn Visnius

Deborah Sabo

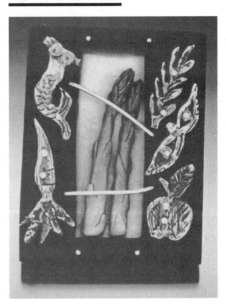

Musical Interpretation, inlaid and riveted, sterling and acrylic, 5" x 3" x 4", 1990. (Violin pin with case necklace in display table = jewelry box set.)

Farmers Prayer, cast and riveted, sterling, acrylic and clay, 1.25" x 2.25", 1990. (Pin with stand in back.)

Photo credit:
Ralph Gabriner

Mythical Threshold, fabricated, copper, sterling, acrylic, shell, pearls, emeralds and cubic zircona, 12" x 3" x 12", 1991. (Mermaid pin with fish earrings, a jewelry box set.)

Mark Alderete

The Return, etched, holloware and cast, brass, nickel, titanium, sterling, jasper and glass, 6" x 6" x 9", 1990.

The Deer Thing, cast, anodized, formed and etched, copper, sterling, wood, gold leaf, marble, nickel, paper and titanium, 16" x 8" x 8", 1991.

Snake Pin, anodized, copper, sterling, titanium, niello and snakeskin, 3" x 4", 1991.

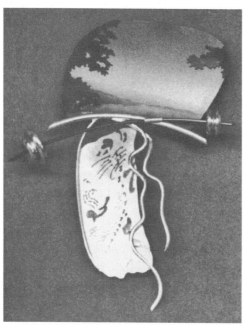

Dichotomy, etched, pierced and anodized, titanium, sterling, niello and copper, 3" x .5" x 4", 1991.

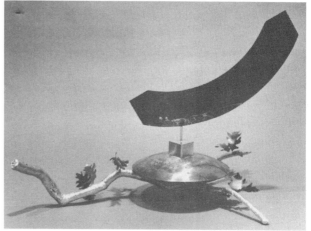

Night in the Gila, formed and anodized, copper, sterling, titanium, wood and gold leaf, 14" x 5" x 12", 1991.

Glenda Rowley

Prince Charming, repousse and chasing, copper, silk and emeralds, 3.5" x 2" x .5", 1990.

The Final Frontier, kaleidoscope, constructed, nickel, sterling, carnelian, amethyst and moonstone, 4" x 2.5" dia, 1990. Photo credit: Charles Lewton-Brain

William Baran-Mickle

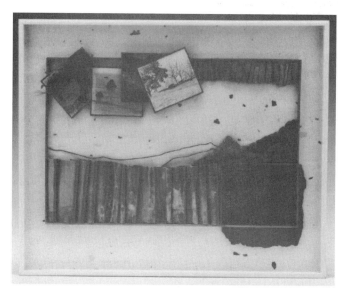

Fiords Past Time, raised, fabricated and painted, brass, nickel, slate, paint, photographs, rice paper and a frame, 20.25" x 16.25", 1989-90.

Transcentric Values, formed, fabricated, carved and painted, wood, glass, nickel, brass and paint, 14.5" x 6" x 20.5", 1990.

A Successful Season: A Memorial, raised, fabricated, carved and painted, copper, brass, Plexiglas, Zerography, wood, paint and mat board, 16.25" x 4.5" x 20.25", 1989.

Photo credit: Bill McDowell

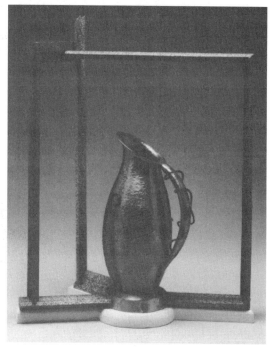

Johan Rhodes: Update to 1989, raised, fabricated, painted and dyed, copper, brass, wood, paint and dye, 16.5" x 11" x 20.5", 1989.

Brian Poor

Coelophysis, fabricated, copper, 7" x 1.5" x 10", 1991.

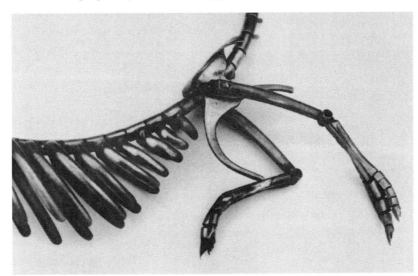

Photo credit:
C.O.D. Cheekz

Coelophysis, detail, fabricated, copper, 7" x 1.5" x 10", 1991.

Tackling The Illuminated Form

by Charles A. Kumnick

What can be so difficult about making an illuminated form? Wire a bulb, stick it

Seven Steps, hot formed, welded, brazed, painted, threaded and bolted, steel, acrylic, brass, copper and electrical components, 24" x 8" x 8", 1991.

in a cardboard box, and plug it in the wall. .... BINGO! .... An illuminated sculpture! ... A MAGICAL FORM!

True, it can be just this simple; or it can be more complicated than you would care to imagine.

Regardless of individual expression, aesthetic orientation or preference of techniques and materials, each artist craftsperson, must acknowledge and satisfy certain functional requirements to eliminate unwanted electrifying results: zaps or sparks. Principle areas of concern include: safety, intent of lighted form, choice of electrical system, lamp bulb type and shape, lamp holder design, switching and wiring.

Safety

If you are unfamiliar with electrical theory, *it is imperative that you seek a licensed electrician for advice and direction before you start experimenting.* Although the actual electrical connections and mechanics are relatively simple, mistakes

Article photo credit: Philip W. Smith Photography

can produce real danger from electrical shock and the potential of fire!

Light Management

Once you have decided to include a light source, you need to define the intent of the light. Do you want this form to serve as a task light (work oriented activity), an ambient light (source of simple room illumination), or to feature the aesthetic and expressive characteristics of your object? How do you want the light to interact with its environment? Do you want a bright projected beam that focuses on a work surface? Or, do you want a soft intimate light that floods a general area, or washes a corner, wall, ceiling, floor? You may prefer to ignore functional constraints and direct light beams focusing on the colors, textures, or other physical features of your piece. Screens, grids, punctures, or textures can be used to project patterns or create special lighting effects.

Clarifying your lighting objectives may simplify subsequent choices about the quantity and quality of light needed, i.e.: system, lamp bulb (size, shape and wattage), and may dictate some of the form constraints: floor, table, wall, ceiling, hanging, portable, etc.

Many systems are capable of generating light for a sculptural form. In this article I will focus on incandescent systems. Basic choices include: common 120 volt AC alternating current, low voltage systems (6-12 volt AC), as well as battery operated, DC, direct current. Electrical components for standard 120 volt AC systems are inexpensive, readily available in most hardware stores, simple to wire, dependable, and offer a wide variety of light management and design versatility.

Tungsten halogen and high intensity 12 volt AC systems require a voltage transformer, but offer intense light at low energy expense. *OUIJA* has a 12 volt AC system

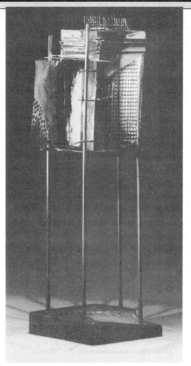

NACCI, welded, brazed, soldered, painted, threaded and bolted, steel, acrylic, brass, copper, pewter and electrical components, 24" x 8.5" x 8.5", 1991.

with a high intensity bulb. The 120-12 volt transformer and the full range dimmer are housed in the box on one of its legs. *MIDNIGHT BLUE* has a 12 volt 50 watt halogen pin bulb with its transformer secured in a vented metal cylinder at the base of a hollow leg. Battery systems (C, D, AA, and AAA) are safe, but are somewhat impractical since the bulb consumes so much current that the batteries have to be continuously replaced or recharged.

Lamp Bulb

Flame, torpedo, bent tip, globe, spot,

Each person must decide for themselves how safety conscious they will be. This article shows one artist's approach to their own studio work. Do not follow it verbatim — decide for yourself on the important issues of health and safety. See page 3.

Candela, threaded, bolted, painted, brazed, cold formed and lathe turned, paper, steel, copper, brass, acrylic and electrical components, 16" x 16" x 8", 1991.

projector, reflector and flood, are descriptions of only some of available incandescent lamp bulbs. Most of these shapes have a rating range from 15 through 100 watts. All 120 volt incandescent bulbs, standard and halogen, that I have used are of the screw design. Battery operated incandescent bulbs can be purchased in screw, bayonet and pin designs.

The tungsten halogen incandescent lamps offer a brilliant white light. Although the 120-12 volt transformer system offers the greatest energy conservation and brightness, the 120 volt lamp bulbs are long lasting and simpler to include.

Most people find a clear bare bulb extremely offensive. If you are not using a "Soft-White" or frosted bulb, it may be desirable to shield the eye from direct contact. A diffusing plane (glass, acrylic or other) can be used to soften glare, add color and create a magical glow. One of the drawbacks of incandescent systems, as compared to the cooler fluorescent tubes, is the generated heat. This heat can burn your skin, blister paint on metal, discolor or singe/ignite paper, plastic, wood and other flammable materials. A broad range of materials can be used to fabricate a "shade," but experimentation may be necessary to insure there's a safe margin of space between the bulb and the shade.

Lamp Holder — Socket

In many cases the socket type and size will be dictated by your choice of bulb.

Most hardware, home centers and electrical supply stores stock brass, porcelain and Bakelite sockets in a wide variety of types and designs. Standard, candelabra or minican bases can easily be incorporated into your design using traditional mechanical fasteners or simple custom applications. Socket bases can also be coupled with "generic lamp parts" (nuts, threaded rods, tube, bends, rotating unions, finials, shade holders or pre-drilled weighted bases) to expedite fabrication or suit design needs.

Switching

The most direct way to turn off a light is yank the cord out of the socket. If you favor a more sophisticated manner, many choices are available.

The simplest switch is a single throw...on-off. This switch can be purchased as part of the socket, or separately, as a unit to be included in a convenient place in the form or on the wire. Push button, slide, toggle and rocker switches can be fastened and wired into a base or creatively installed into a sculptural element. *CANDELA* has a Radio Shack toggle switch anchored into an acrylic disk bolted to a fabricated brass cone.

Variable light levels can be achieved either by matching 3-way bulbs and sockets or by investing in a specific dimmer switch. Two and three step dimmers (100%, 70%, 30%) can be found as a "touch-on," an in-line unit, a wired remote unit and a radio activated device. Full range dimmers can be on the cord, a wired remote unit or incorporated into the structure of the sculpture. *CIRUS* has a radio activated three level switch which can be operated from fifty feet away. If fully enclosed, inexpensive wall dimmers can be used with very satisfactory results. *SEVEN STEPS* and *NACCI* each have full range dimmer controls incorporated into the base.

Because most dimmer switches, and many other electrical components, are heat sensitive, bulb proximity must be a consideration if you are enclosing these electrical components. Venting the form, or allowing for convecting air passage, can extend the life of all parts of your construction.

Wiring

One of the easiest decisions is the choice of wire. For most applications, standard lamp cord (18 gauge, two wire, stranded copper wire) is adequate. A reoccurring aesthetic problem is that this cord must run from the power source through your sculpture to the bulb. Although this "tail" is an honest extension of an electrical device there is no reason to feature it; hence it becomes one of the compositional decisions. Cords come in a wide variety of colors to match almost any scheme; black, white, brown and clear are most available. In the sculpture *CIRUS*, I used a ladder form to incorporate the power path. In *MIDNIGHT BLUE*, I slid the wire from the transformer housing up through a hollow support leg. In *OUIJA*, I used the shade suspension wires and the painted steel legs to carry the current.

Plug

The simplest solution I have found for a plug is an "Easy On" plug. It is a paintable plastic device that slips onto any 18 gauge lamp cord with minimal assembly and no tools. The drawback is that these plugs are not polarized to differentiate the hot line from the neutral spade.

Stability

Structural stability is always a construction factor for sculptors and object makers. In electrical devices, it is a prime concern. To avoid user accidents, and to minimize damage to delicate electrical components, carefully consider a very stable stance for your form.

Replacement of Parts

All parts wear out sooner or later. Unless you intend to discard your piece when the bulb burns out, you must make accommodations for replacement. A well designed lamp should make allowances for all electrical parts to be replaced: wiring, switches, plugs, sockets and transformers. When wiring and installing these electrical parts insure that all of your electrical connections are carefully insulated and not touching any metal parts. Wire nuts,

Ouija, raised, hot formed, lathe turned, welded, brazed, electroplated and painted, acrylic, 24k, copper, brass, sterling silver and electrical components, 28" x 18" x 12", 1990.

heat-shrink insulating tube and electrical tape is very effective at maintaining this safe posture. You may even wish to secure all wiring with electrical solder. To avoid electrical shocks and protect expensive lamp components, a fuse can be wired into the system to avoid damage from a short circuit.

In all cases, Underwriter Lab Approved (UL) electrical components should be used.

Additional Electrical Information

There are numerous books and pamphlets available that present volumes of technical information. Many of these texts are confusing if you have never attempted electrical wiring. It is best to contact someone with experience, a licensed electrician or perhaps an instructor at a neighboring high school or college.

Certainly, the ultimate way to address many of these concerns is to just DO IT, and see what happens. "COMMON SENSE"

and your own experience with common lighting fixtures and sculpture will guide you through most decisions. After you complete one light, you will know whether it stirs your amps enough to try another.

The objective of this article is not to paralyze you with confusing technological fears, or to supply you with all you need to know, but simply to heighten your awareness toward basic considerations and pique your interest at the potential of including a light in a form.

GO ON! DO IT! LIGHT UP YOUR LIFE!

Midnight Blue, table light, fabricated, raised. hot formed, lathe turned, welded and painted, steel, copper, brass, acrylic, sterling silver and electrical components, 25" x 18" x 15", 1990.

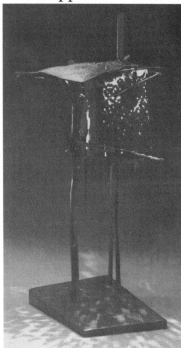

Other Bound, hot formed, welded, brazed, painted, threaded, bolted and assembled, steel, wood, acrylic, brass and electrical components, 20" x 9" x 6", 1992.

Charles Kumnick, assistant professor of Art, teaches Sculpture and Jewelry Design at Trenton State College.

For the past two years his studio work has been supported by a Trenton State College Project Grant, Distinguished Research Award, 1990-92 and by a Crafts Fellowship from the Pennsylvania Council on the Arts, 1991.

Information Age Jewelry

by Vernon Reed

From prehistoric times to the present, jewelry has been identified with <u>hardware</u> of some kind, configured in <u>3-dimensional space</u>. The technologies of the information revolution afford a new possibility: cybernetic jewelry. Here a significant part is the <u>software</u>, manifesting in the <u>time dimension</u>. In this article, I will endeavor to give the reader some sense of what a cybernetic

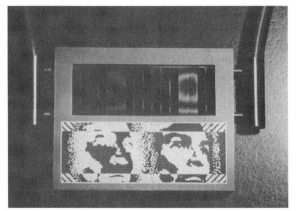

Twin Paradox Melt Down, various, see text, microcomputer, software, LCD, titanium and acrylic, 2.5" x 3.25" x .5", 1989.

jewel is, by describing the creation of one. The cybernetic neckpiece *TWIN PARADOX MELTDOWN* is typical of the kind of work I am doing now, and, will serve as a demonstration piece.

Cybernetic jewelry consists of three major parts: (1) the case, typically made of metal and/or plastic; (2) the computer and output hardware, typically a CMOS microcomputer driving a liquid crystal display; (3) the software, which runs on the computer and controls the configuration of the output device in real time. I will concentrate on the last two areas, since much information is readily available on working

Each person must decide for themselves how safety conscious they will be. This article shows one artist's approach to their own studio work. Do not follow it verbatim — decide for yourself on the important issues of health and safety. See page 3.

with metal and plastic.

The visual effect of cybernetic jewelry is time-based, like music or video, as opposed to being spatially oriented, like sculpture. Given this, I wanted to create a piece which would relate to the issue of time on several levels. The most powerful evocation of time-based phenomena is the relativistic dilation of time at near-light speed. This was aptly illustrated by Einstein with the twin paradox, where the twin traveling at light speed hardly ages while the other grows old and dies. Having decided on subject matter, I also decided that I wanted this piece to look like a machine, making no effort to integrate it with human contours, as I had always done previously.

I started by designing proportions for the case sufficient to enclose the computer system and batteries. I fabricated it out of black acrylic. Then I made front and back plates out of titanium, and connectors for the rubber tube out of gold-plated brass. The raw data for the face image were scanned from a photo, and modified with image processing and paint software, running on an Apple Macintosh computer. The resulting image was reduced and turned into a photographic negative, which I employed to anodize the titanium using standard photo-anodizing techniques. The case assembled from these parts was then ready to contain the computer hardware.

Twin Paradox Melt Down, inside view.

The computer in *TWIN PARADOX MELT-DOWN* is a Motorola 68HC805 and contains on-chip 4 kilobytes of EEPROM memory (this is computer memory that does not lose data when power is removed, very important), along with three bit-addressable input/output (I/O) ports. This large number of output lines makes it possible to drive a liquid crystal display (LCD) directly, without employing extra driver chips. The clock speed of the computer is extremely slow, 32 kilohertz, in order to minimize current drain.

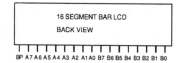

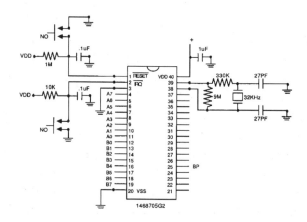

As space is always a limiting factor in designing wearable systems, I do not use a circuit board for the computer chip, which comes in a 40-pin DIP package. Instead, I socket the chip and solder such ancillary components as resistors, capacitors and crystal directly to the leads of the socket, resulting in the smallest possible package. The interrupt request line is carried to the outside world as input, for run time program mode selection. I use two entire output ports, plus one bit of a third port, to drive the LCD which serves as my output device.

Front plane electrode pattern

Back plane electrode pattern

I design and fabricate the LCD's for my cybernetic jewels, so I am able to use whatever images or patterns I desire. For this piece, I wanted a fairly large display with a linear pattern, superimposed on a color field background. LCD's are basically electronically controlled light valves, and work by means of selectively polarizing and depolarizing the light which is reflected or transmitted through them. The areas which perform this action are defined by the overlapping of transparent electrode patterns on the front and back glass plates. The glasses create a cell containing a thin (0.0001") film of the twisted-nematic liquid crystal material, which changes polarization in response to electrical signals.

I created the artwork for the electrode patterns using Superpaint running on a Macintosh. This artwork was then reduced and turned into photographic negatives, which were employed to photoetch the electrodes from a transparent, electroconductive, indium-tin oxide layer on the glass. I then assembled the LCD in my "clean room" using a suite of specialized equipment, such as a molecular-alignment buffer, high precision screen printer, vacuum fill chamber and various ovens. Wires were attached to the finished display with electroconductive epoxy and these wires were soldered to the computer chip's socket.

Clean room for LCD fabrication.

All the work on *TWIN PARADOX MELT-DOWN* up to this point served to provide a matrix, or substrate, to support the feature that makes cybernetic jewelry truly revolutionary: namely the software program which runs on the computer. This software instructs the computer to perform specific sequences of tasks which control the LCD in real time. The dynamic visual aspect of the LCD can assume a great number of states, depending on the instructions being sent from the computer, and these instructions, and thus the appearance of the piece, can be changed without altering the hardware in any way. This terminates jewelry's historical identification with hardware, and points to potentials that my current, rather crude devices can only hint at.

Since the 68HC805 has only 4k (!) of memory, using high level languages like pascal or basic is simply out of the question, but I do not really want to program in assembly language. The solution was to commission the creation of a proprietary computer language I call DSKTRN, which is extremely compact and is optimized for controlling a direct-drive LCD. This language is written in assembler and consists of a section of macro handling code, coupled with macro instructions which perform specific operations on the LCD, such as shift right or left, flash, etc.

Programs for my cybernetic jewels are written using an integrated editor and cross-assembler from P & E Microcomputer Systems Inc., running on an IBM PC. This very slick package enables me to write programs and assemble them with a minimum of fuss. Debugging is accomplished

```
MAINLOOP: BCLR  RQS100,STAT1,MLOP,BRANCH IF NO 100 MS REQ
          JSR   DISPLAY
MLOP1:    WAIT                ;WAIT FOR NEXT TIME INERRUPT
          BRA   MAINLOP  ;STAY IN THIS LOOP FOREVER
DISPLAY:  BCLR  RQS100,STAT1   ;CLEAR THE 100 MS FLAG
          DEC   TIMEW      ;DECREMENT TIME
          BNE   EXIT       ;LEAVE IF NOT ZERO
          LDA   TIMEREG    ;GET VALUE
          STA   TIMEW      ;PUT IN WORKING LOCATION
          DEC   NUMTIMES   ;CHECK IF ALL ARE DONE
          BNE   DIS1       ;SKIP THE MOVE TO NEXT BLOCK
          LDA   DESTIN1    ;
          ADD   DESTIN2    ;COMPLETE CHECK FOR NEXT
          BNE   NEWLOAD    ;LOAD NEW BLOCK IN DESTIN1
DESTIN2
          JSR   LOADNEXT   ;LOAD NEXT BLOCK IF DESTINATION =0
          RTS              ;RETURN TO CALLER
NEWLOAD:  JSR   LOADNEW    ;LOAD A NEW DESTINATION SET
EXIT:     RTS              ;RETURN TO CALLER
```

with a Motorola EVM emulator, a special computer board which acts like a 68HC805, but which has on-board diagnostic capabilities. I hook this board to the PC through a parallel port, and attach a target LCD circuit to it. Program downloading and EVM control is accomplished with another P & E Microcomputer Systems Inc. product, a terminal emulation program, which provides a very powerful user interface to the debugging monitor on the EVM. What all this means is that I can write programs and test them before I load them into the computer which will reside in a jewel.

The program running on *TWIN PARA-DOX MELTDOWN*, DSKTRN 17, was writ-

ten in four modules. Each module has a distinctive "feel," e.g. a rapid, staccato movement in the LCD, or a more lyrical and soothing motion, etc. These modules can be chosen by the wearer to create a

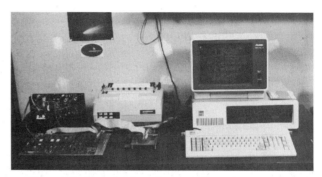
Software development system.

mood in time as well as space. This selection is made by pushing the interrupt request switch on the bottom of the case, which steps the program through all available choices.

After writing and debugging DSKTRN 17, I loaded it into the EEPROM memory of the 68HC805 chip and inserted this chip into the socket with all the ancillary components and LCD attached to it. This entire unit was then placed in the case and connected to the lithium batteries, and the back plate was attached with screws, completing the piece.

I hope the foregoing has given you some feel for the possibilities afforded, when we embrace the fantastic capabilities of the new information age technologies. The future is now.

For further information:

Reed, Vernon; *Cybernetic Jewelry: Ornament for the Information Age*, "The Visual Computer," 1988, #4, p 27-34.

Reed, Vernon; *Beyond Hardware: Jewelry for a Brave New World*, "Ornament," winter 1987, 10 (4), p 40-45.

Reed, Vernon; *Cybernetic Jewelry: A Systems Approach*, "Metalsmith," winter 1987, p 30-33.

I am a computer artist, working with wearable systems. My formal training is in experimental psychology. My primary interest lies in the extension of human experience into information space, as defined by the synergistic confluence of computer and communication technologies. I consider my current work to be rather simple, proof-of-concept experiments for the larger body of work I have outlined in my theoretical writings.

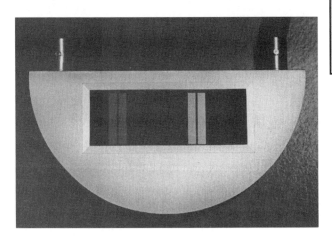

Radio Saturn, various, microcomputer, software, LCD, titanium and acrylic, 2.5" x 4.5" x .5", 1991. (The LCD is in constant motion.)

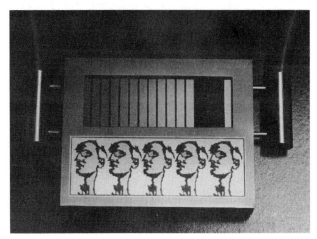

Alien Day, various, microcomputer, software, LCD, titanium and acrylic, 2.5" x 3.25" x .5", 1989. (The LCD is in constant motion.)

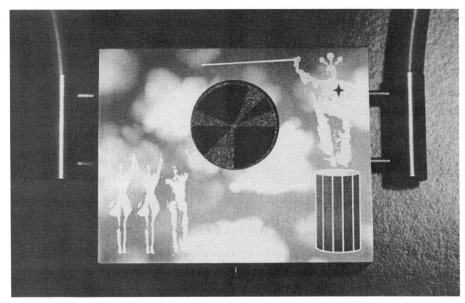

The Magus, various, microcomputer, software, LCD, titanium and acrylic, 2.5" x 3.2" x .5", 1990.

Helen Mason

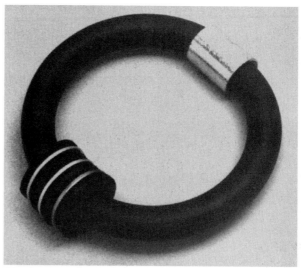

Neckpiece, fabricated, rubber and steel, 7" x 7", 1991.

Brooch, fabricated and woven, Teflon, sterling silver, rubber and steel, 3.25" x 3.25", 1990.

Brooch, fabricated and woven, Teflon, anodized aluminum, rubber and steel, 3.25" x 3.25", 1990.

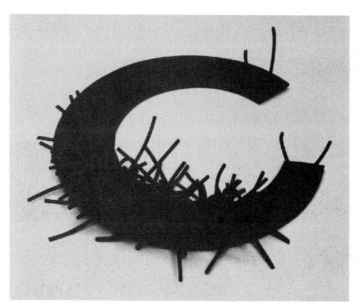

Neckpiece, knotted and fabricated, rubber and sterling silver, 10" x 9", 1990.

Photo credit: Bobby Hansson

Marjorie Schick

Wall Sculpture with Brooch, constructed, painted wood, 16" x 4.5" x 13", 1991.

Wall Sculpture with Brooch, constructed, painted wood, 16.5" x 3" x 16.5", 1991.

Collar, constructed, painted papier-mache, 16" x 2" x 16", 1991.

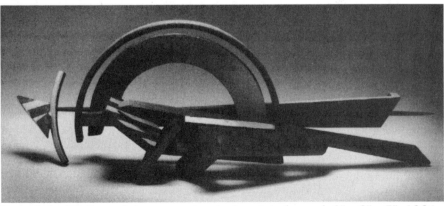

Brooch for Wall, sculpture, constructed, painted wood, 9" x 3" x 5", 1991.

Photo credit: Joel Degan

Kathlean Gahagan
Candace Miller

Candace Miller, earrings, plastic clay, 1" x 1", 1991.*

Candace Miller, brooch, plastic clay, 3" x 3", 1991.*

Candace Miller, brooch, plastic clay, 3" x 2", 1991.*

*Photo credit: David LaPlantz
°Photo credit: Robert Liu

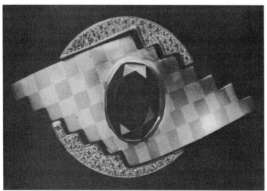

Intersection Series, hematite, cubic zirconium, sterling silver and nickel, 3.5" x 2.25", 1991.°

Intersection Necklace, sterling silver, nickel and tourmaline beads, 3.5" x 3.5" x 18", 1990.°

Veronica Szalus

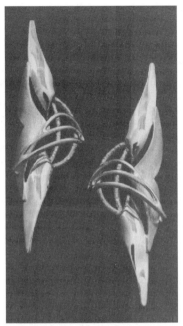

Wing Earrings, cast and fabricated, sterling, 2.5 " x .75" x .5", 1989.

Corkscrew Necklace, fabricated, sterling, black onyx and hematite, center: 3.25" x 2" x .75", 1989.

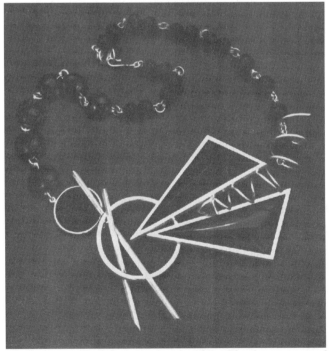

Corkscrew II, fabricated, sterling, black onyx and citrine, center: 5.5" x 4" x .75", 1991.

James Malenda

Station Study I, fabricated and painted, aluminum, copper and paint, 48" x 10" x 24", 1991.

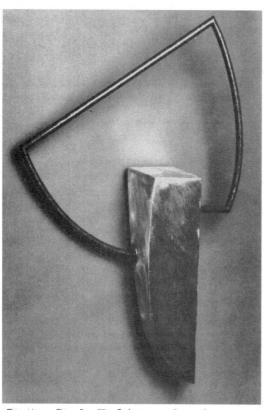

Station Study II, fabricated and painted, aluminum, copper and paint, 24" x 7" x 30", 1991.

Station Study I, detail, fabricated and painted, aluminum, copper and paint, 1991.

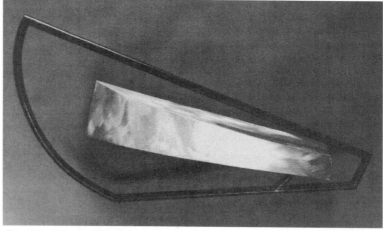

Photo credit: Jeff Unger

Station Study III, fabricated and painted, aluminum, copper and paint, 30" x 10" x 18", 1991.

Lisa Bernfield Ben-Zeev

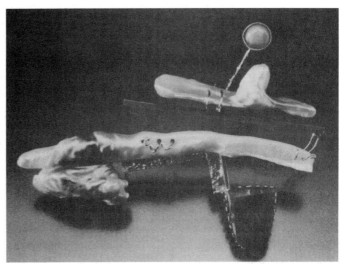

Brooch, 14k, biwa pearls, boulder opal and moonstone, 2.5" x 3" x .5", 1991.

Brooch, 14k yellow and white gold, sterling, aluminum flashing, steel, Roman glass and a pearl, 2.5" x 2.5" x 1.5".

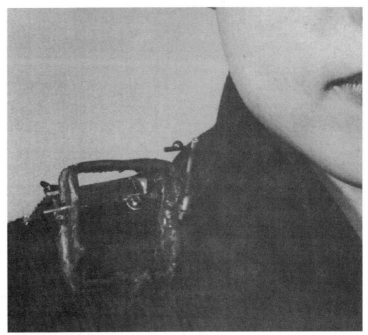

Shoulder Piece, 14k yellow and white gold, sterling, steel flashing, aluminum flashing, boulder opal, pearl and copper, 3" x 3.5" x 2".

Making Myths

by Judith Hoffman

Making art is a particular style is sometimes a difficult proposition for me. I could look at a lot of different people's work, love it, and rush home inspired to make something like that. If I followed all these impulses I would be making versions of other people's things all the time. I do think a certain amount of imitation is okay. The best way for me to acquire knowledge of a new technique is to make something in a style that I admire. But I could never come to feel I had a style of my own if I were always so influenced by other people's work.

There are things that are unique in each person. We all experience and view the world in different ways. There is an essential core of being in me that is unlike anyone else. I want to tap that uniqueness and use it in my jewelry and sculpture. By getting a sense of that inner self I can develop a style that is mine. The personal connection I feel with my imagery makes it easier for me to continue to work when I am in a slump and don't feel like doing anything. I have found that writing, recording my dreams and reading are good methods to become more aware of my essential self. I use all three techniques at different times to collect material that illustrates my inner self.

Over the years I have combined this material to form my own myths. These myths explain the world for me and provide me with the imagery for my work. For example, one of my first writings was about sinking into water and being transformed into a fish. It was my fantasy of what death might be like. Since I did that writing I have used a lot of fish and creatures who are part fish, part people in my work. They are often suspended in space, surrounded by stars and sea creatures. These fish people have come to symbolize a complicated set of ideas for me. MAN FISH WHO BREATHES THE NIGHT was made as a companion for an earlier woman book person I made. He is complementary to her. She is all human, while he is part fish, part human. She expresses her inner life, while he goes into the sea to find knowledge of mysterious things. He is the one who can travel into forbidden places, deep under the sea and find answers to our hardest questions. Why do people die? Where do they go? What is it like? Could we send them messages? There is a book in his chest with three silver pages which show a little house under a moon. The house draws the Man Fish back to the earth after he has been in the sea.

These ideas are closely connected with writings I have done. But other myths I have made for myself don't have any counterpart in the work I do. And some of the things I make don't seem connected to the myths. I just enjoy the process of making them. I am sure a connection exists between most of the work and the myths, even when it is not apparent.

Writings

My writings are the main source of material for my myths. They are often repetitive and sometimes they seem silly when I look back at them. I write in a stream of consciousness style that pays no attention to rules of grammar or style.

Often my writings are full of visual imagery. I think I get a lot of imagery because I usually describe things or events rather than sticking with ideas or feelings. I also personify things into animals or objects. I'm not sure why this happens, but there seems to be a connection between personification and liking children's stories and myths and legends.

Occasionally a whole writing just comes into my head and I write it down. These are my favorites. Over the years I have begun to see themes that reoccur, like the fish.

Dreams

My dreams have been a good source of material for my myths. Dreams have an interior logic that I find whimsical and enchanting. It seems best to just record them without trying to understand them. Years ago I spent a lot of time writing down dreams and then writing about what they seemed to mean. When I looked back at my interpretations, even a few months later, I saw that they were complete bunk. Now I prefer to see dreams as messages from another part of my life, a part I don't have conscious access to. I write them down to cherish the dream logic and the imagery, but I no longer try to analyze their meaning. By honoring them in this way I allow the dream logic to enter into my working vocabulary without filtering through my intellect.

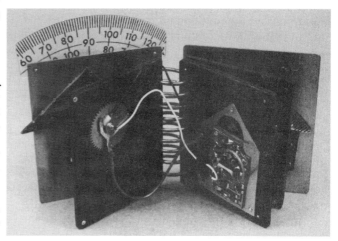

Instruction Manual for the Moon, fabricated, brass, Plexiglas and found objects, 2" x 4.25" x 2.25", 1989.

Reading

There are a few books I have read that I find completely enchanting. They hold images that seem to resonate with imagined things from my childhood or my dreams. Ultimately I think a lot of these ideas are "in the air" or in our collective unconscious.

A book by Italo Calvino called <u>Cosmicomics</u> is my all time favorite. It contains 12 short stories. The first story is about a time when the moon was close enough to the earth for people to climb up on it. When the moon passed close by the ocean, little jellyfish, crabs and other sea creatures floated in the air between the earth and the moon. After I did the writing about becoming a part fish, part human creature I have been visualizing fish people in settings where they were existing with

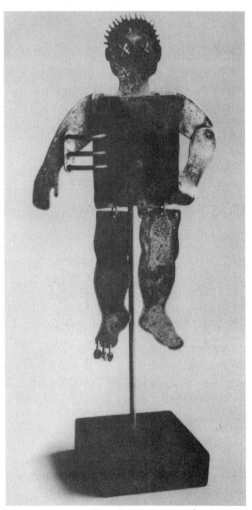

Man moon - Go, heat treated, copper plated and fabricated, brass and found objects, .75" x 3" x 4.75", 1989. (His left hand holds the book in his chest shut.)

stars, fish and sea creatures. Finding Calvino's similar description of people floating almost weightlessly in the air between the earth and moon with little sea creatures around them was a real treat for me.

Suggestions for Implementing these Ideas

Writing

Write in a quiet place with no distractions. Don't try to write literature and don't try to decide what's good or bad. Just let the ideas flow. Write down whatever comes into your head and worry about spelling and punctuation later. Remember you don't "ever" have to show what you write to anyone. The main purpose of the writing is to help you to connect with your inner life. You may not think there is anything of interest in what you write, but don't give up too soon. After you have been writing for a while, go back through everything and look for themes that reoccur.

Some people don't ever enjoy writing. If the writing doesn't work, you might want to make a collage or drawing to illustrate your images and feelings. Try not to judge whatever you do. Not only is it private, you don't have to decide if it's good or bad.

Ideas to help start you writing:

Write about an early childhood memory; one you feel was an important event that shaped your life.

Write about what moves you. What do you find important about life? What are you struggling to understand?

Write about an important object you remember from your childhood. This could be a stone you found, a favorite toy that had great meaning, or even a person who was important.

Write about something you have made. Imagine it can talk to you. Ask it questions. Why does it exist?

Write about a piece you have made as if you could enter into it. Describe the interior. How do you feel there?

Be aware of any event that you feel an important connection with. You might see something on television or just hear a bird song that reminds you of a childhood event. All these things can be written about to help clarify what they mean to you.

Recording Dreams

When you first wake up in the morning, lie still, keep your eyes closed and try to remember your dreams. If nothing comes at first, try to get just an image. Sometimes it helps to think of people close to you (i.e., "Did I dream about my mother? My brother? Etc.) Sometimes it takes days of trying just to get a little start. When you have the dreams in mind, open your eyes, move as little as possible, reach for the pencil and pad you keep by your bed, and write everything down. I often list the general subject of each dream in the margin before I start writing. I tend to forget the later dream subjects by the time I have written the first ones. After writing your dreams regularly for a while, you will find that you remember more and more.

Read your dreams occasionally. I'm often amazed at what I forget. Look for reoccurring themes that might point the way to something you could write about.

Stay Open to Things

Whether you get ideas from writing, dreams, books or chance happenings, things will at times seem important in mysterious ways. They may vaguely remind you of some other time or place. These events can be cherished, recorded and used to help clarify your inner being.

Remember, all this should be fun. Don't take it too seriously. We're only here for a short time. There is no definitive explanation for why we're alive or what we're supposed to be doing. Enjoy the process.

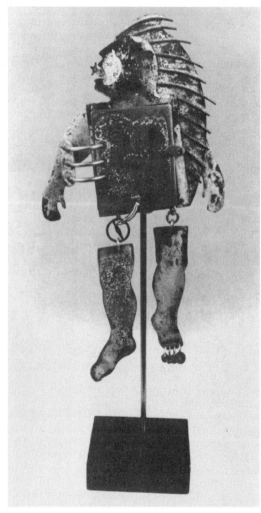

Man Fish Who Breathes the Night, heat treated, copper plated and fabricated, silver, brass and watch parts, .25" x 4" x 5.25", 1989. (The book in his chest opens to reveal 3 pierced pages.)

I got my MFA at San Jose State and am now living in San Francisco with my husband and cat. I use jewelry techniques to make small sculptures and jewelry with silver, copper and brass, and some found objects.

Thomas Mann

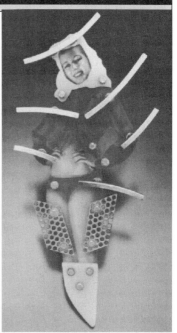

Pin-up #2, silver, nickel, bronze, brass, colored Lucite and postcard, 2" x 5", 1991.

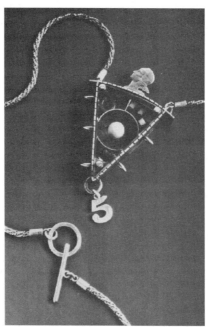

#5, silver, nickel, bronze, brass, Lucite and found objects, 2" x 3" x .5", 1990.

Pin-up #1, silver, nickel, bronze, brass, colored Lucite and post-card, 2" x 5", 1991.

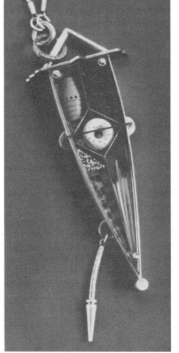

Collage Box Neckpiece, silver, nickel, bronze, brass, Lucite and found objects, 1" x 6" x .5", 1990.

Photo credti: Will Crocker

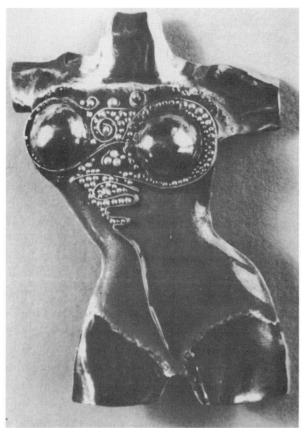

Nancy Moyer

Orange Torso Brooch, enamel, granulation, gold doublee, formed and dapped, fine silver and enamel, 3.5" x 2.5", 1990.

Warrior Torso Pendant, fabrication and enameling, fine silver and enamels, 3.5" x 2.5" x 13" chain, 1991.

Eric Marlow

Sarcophaguy, cast and fabricated, bronze, silver and marble. Copyright 1992 Eric Marlow

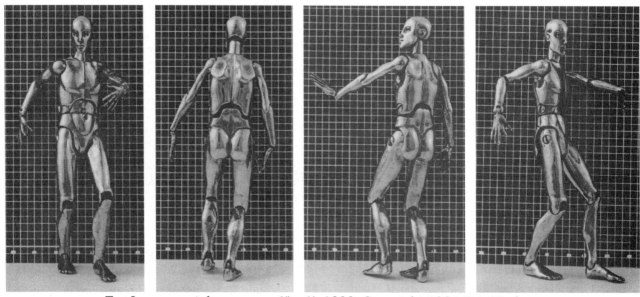

Too Loose, cast, bronze, ea: 1" x 1', 1990. Copyright 1991 Eric Marlow

Karen Pierce

Dreaming of the Lotus Keeper, formed and fabricated, copper and paint, 32" x 5"dia, 1991. Photo credit: Ray Garcia

Neumann People, formed, fabricated, Ashante cast, carved and painted, copper, brass, bronze, shibuichi and jelutong, 25" x 25" x 32", 1991. Photo credit: Robert Sherwood

Robly A. Glover

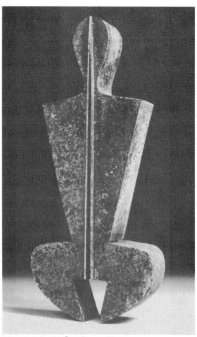

*Venus of the Furrow, con-
structed, brass with patina, 8" x
3.5" x 1.5", 1991.*

*Matristic Libation Vessel, constructed,
brass with patina, 9" x 6" x 1.5", 1991.*

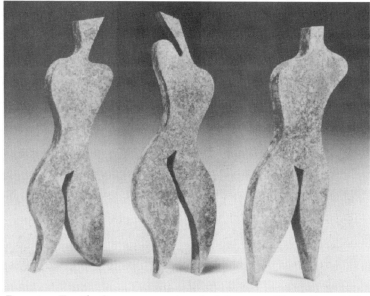

*Dancing Fertile Graces, constructed, brass with patina, 12" x
4" x 1", 1990.*

Nancy Slagle

Stick Pin, constructed, silver, 4" x 1.25" x .25", 1990.

*Decanter with Cups, constructed, sterling silver, 4" x 3" x 7', 1991.**

*New Mexico Blue - Peggy Sue, constructed, sterling silver, wood and paint, 7' x 4" x 7.5", 1989.**

Lilith, brooch, constructed and roller printed, silver, 3" x 1.5" x .25", 1991.

Photo credit: Robert Suddarth

149

Enid Kaplan

Body Talk, body sculpture, constructed and forged, copper and brass wire, 24" x 10" x 26", 1991.

All Roads Lead to Roam (Home), constructed, stone, sterling silver, brass, onyx, niobium and paint, 18" x 20" x 8", 1991. (Figure is a single earring which also fits into the arch as a pin.)

Photo crdit: Guy L'Heureux

Doppleganger (Second Self), brooch, fabricated, 14k, moonstone, tourmaline, sterling silver, ebony, shell and radio circuit, 3" x 2.5" x 1", 1991.

Village Elders, earrings, cast and constructed, sterling silver, carnelian, bone, copper and brush, 3" x 1.25" x .5", 1991.

Karen S. Bournias

The Offering, cast and manipulated, sterling silver, 18k gold and coral, 3" x 2" x 1.5", 1991.

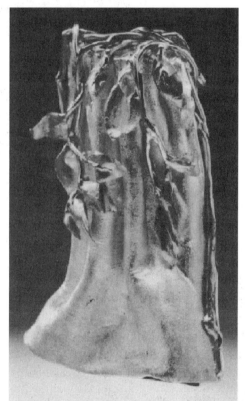

Fabric & Vine, cast and formed, sterling silver and 10k gold, 3" x 2.5" x 1.5", 1991.

Fabric & Arborvitae, cast and formed, sterling silver and 10k gold, 3" x 3.5" x 1.5", 1991.

Photo credit: Richard Pottieger

Electro-forming: Lightweight Magic

by Karen and Frederic Duclos

Of the numerous metalsmithing methods, none is as unique as the magical process of electroforming. Electroforming, as its name implies, employs electrochemical principles to form a sound metallic body around a temporary core. This core may be a low-melting point wax, a dissolvable resin, a chemically removable metal or other temporary matrix.

The electroforming process was first developed in 1838 by Morris Hartman Von Jacobi in Russia. Technology has advanced greatly since 1838. In fact, it's now possible to buy a computer controlled system that will mass produce electroformed items. This article will focus on the "old school" techniques, allowing the craftsperson to experiment without investing an exorbitant amount of money. We wish to give the

Frederic Duclos, Large Twist, electroformed, silver, 1.75" x 1.5" x 1", 1991.

Article photo credit: Stu Preston

Each person must decide for themselves how safety conscious they will be. This article shows one artist's approach to their own studio work. Do not follow it verbatim -- decide for yourself on the important issues of health and safety. See page 3.

individual artist an overview of the unique process of electroforming. This is not intended to be a "how-to" guide. Rather, it is written out of eight years of specific experience. The same results may be achieved with numerous alterations.

We started AG Artwear, Inc., after extensive research in the fashion jewelry market. We found a niche for high quality designer pieces at a more conservative cost than other lines. By electroforming, we created an outstanding line of bold, beautiful sterling for a fraction of the cost of more conventional manufacturing methods.

Silver, with its unique characteristics and relatively low cost, will be the choice metal in this article. Jewelry, the primary work of our studio, will also be used as the example.

The art of electroforming may be divided into six steps: design, mandrel preparation, electro-conductivity, electroforming, finishing and decorative accents.

Design

Electroforming is a method used for creating highly sculptural designs that cannot be produced by other means inexpensively. It allows the artist to fabricate multiple pieces of a limited production at a relatively low cost.

Because the silver is evenly applied around the core, like an outer shell, it is much lighter than a cast piece. Thus, the artist saves on metal costs, while preserving the inherent value of a sterling piece as opposed to a plated piece. Even more importantly, the jewelry is light enough to be comfortably worn by the final customer.

Simple designs that can be mass produced by stamping or casting, without weight concerns, should not be considered for electroforming. However, the initial costs for electroforming are significantly lower than the set-up costs of those two manufacturing procedures. electroforming is best applied to more complicated and sculptural designs that can take full advantage of all of this method's benefits.

Original design models can be made out of virtually any material. Wax is commonly used, as well as plaster, clay, wood and resin.

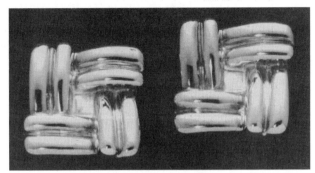

Frederic and Karen Duclos, Square Knot Earrings, electroformed, silver, 1.5" x 1.5" x .5", 1988.

Various mold materials may be used to reproduce your design. These include metal molds, vulcanized molds and regular rubber molds. Mold shrinkage is not a major concern, as the piece regains some size as the metal shell forms around the matrix.

Mandrel Preparation

The raw materials from which the mandrel (core) is made must be given careful consideration. Wax and resin are good choices because they can be removed from the pieces chemically. Additional factors to consider are: melting point, flexibility and the toxicity of the mandrel. Each artist needs to research their own media and decide which materials will be most compatible with their ultimate goals.

Because electroforming occurs directly over a mandrel, any imperfections such as bumps, imperfect texture, holes and deep undercuts will be reproduced, even emphasized, by this process. Great care must be given to prepare the mandrel properly to prevent any defects. The final piece will only be as good as its original.

Electro-conductivity

The coating used to make the mandrel electro-conductive must be compatible with the mandrel material. If a metallized plastic is chosen, it will make the piece conductible. Epoxy resins mixed with common metallic powders, such as graphite, bronze or silver, are the simplest way of achieving this. Conductive inks or lacquers may be applied by brushing the substance over the object, by hand or airbrush, or, by carefully dipping the object. Remember, the goal is to achieve a smooth and even distribution of the lacquer over the object. This is a critical part of the process.

Silver mirroring is another method of making mandrels conductive. However, the toxic waste generated by this process and the additional safety precautions necessary are not justified for a limited production run.

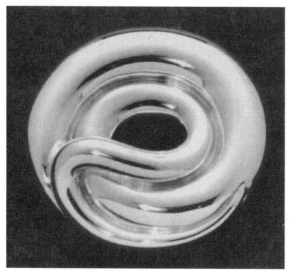

Frederic and Karen Duclos, Swirl Brooch, electroformed, sterling, 2" x 2" x .5", 1990.

Baths

The most commonly used electroforming metals are copper, nickel, silver and gold. Plating baths of these metals are available from any large plating company.

Electroforming a specific jewelry item may employ one or more plating baths of different metals to achieve the desired results.

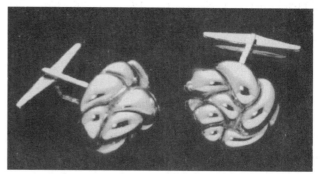

Frederic Duclos, Knotted Cuff Links, electroformed, sterling, .75" x .75" x .5", 1991.

Some technical aspects of an electroforming bath include: temperature, pH, current density, agitation, anode/cathode ratios, anode/cathode distance, acidification, hardness, tensile stress, compression stress, hardness and specific gravity.

The operation, maintenance and technical aspects of carrying out an electroforming process are beyond the scope of this article.

Finishing

The ordinary two step buffing method, red rouge and tripoli, has been replaced by high-tech, controlled velocity finishing machines. The choice of buffing media is extensive and results in different finishes: synthetic plastics for cutting, ceramic for fineness and wood for coloring, etc.

If the mandrel has already been removed before the buffing process, care must be taken not to damage the pieces. If the pieces are not hollowed out before buffing, the temperature from buffing friction might become high enough for the pieces to change shape. Be careful.

Decorative Accents

Fourteen, 18 and 24 karat gold-brush plating is easily applied to finished pieces. Sand-blasting may be done to achieve a matte finish. However, if there are any defects or holes on the piece's surface, the pressure can cause it to crack. Different patinas, such as antiquing, can be applied to the surface, along with common metal treatments creating an array of extraordinary finishes.

In conclusion, electroforming allows the creation of beautiful lasting pieces that will continue to amaze the ultimate consumer because of their weightlessness and reasonable cost.

The balance of art and technology is truly achieved through this unique method of producing outstanding jewelry and objects d'art.

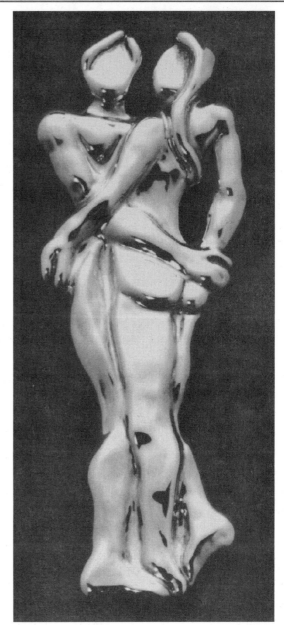

Frederic and Karen Duclos, Dancers Brooch, electroformed, silver, 5.75" x 2.25" x .5", 1990.

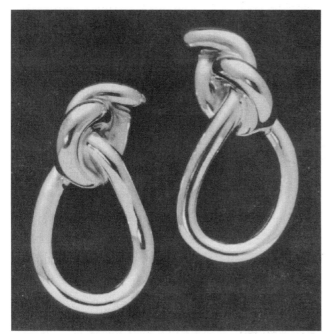

Frederic Duclos, Open Loop Knot Earrings, electroformed, silver, 2.25" x 1.5" x .75", 1992.

Frederic Jean Duclos descended from a family of talented fashion accessory designers. His parents founded the largest shoe factory in Europe in the 1950's.

Karen is from California where she sharpened her natural marketing skills and started importing a variety of women's fashion accessories.

Wynona Alexander

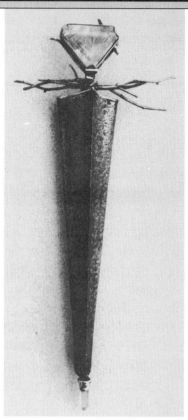

Cache I, brooch, cast and fabricated, copper, sterling, 14k, bronze, rutilated quartz and topaz, 8" x 2.5" x 1.25", 1991.

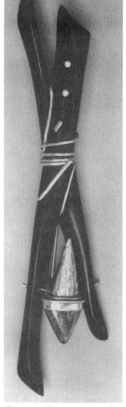

Fence Fragment II, fabricated and etched, sterling, tourmalated quartz and ebony, 8" x 3" x 1", 1991.

Fence Fragment I, fabricated and etched, sterling silver, e b o n y , tourmalated quartz and sapphire, 8" x .5" x 1", 1991.

Cache II, brooch, cast and fabricated, copper, sterling, 14k, bronze, rutilated quartz and topaz, 8" x 2" x 1.25", 1991.

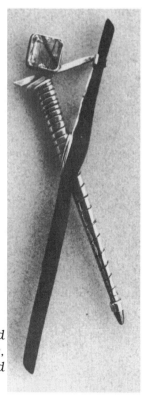

Fence Fragment III, fabricated and etched, sterling, ebony, hematite and tourmalated quartz, 8" x 3.5" x 1", 1991.

Michael Barr

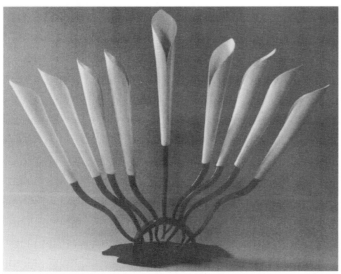

Chanukah Lamp, forged and formed, sterling silver, iron and steel, 8" x 3" x 6", 1989.

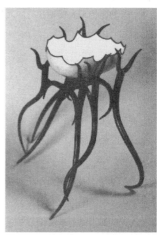

Salt Cellar #12, forged and raised, sterling silver, iron and steel, 4.5" x 3" x 5.5", 1989.

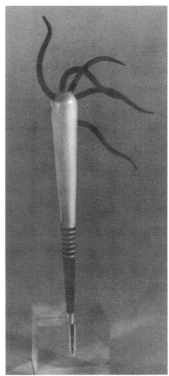

Thumb Tack #53, forged and constructed, sterling silver, iron and steel, 2" x .75" x 3", 1990.

Thumb Tack #47, forged with inlay, sterling silver and steel, 2.5" x .5" x 3.75", 1990.

Fiona Coenen-Winer

Untitled, ring, cast and fabricated, sterling silver, 1" x .75" x 1", 1992.

Untitled, bracelet, cast and anodized, sterling silver and aluminum, 3" x .5" x 2.5", 1992.

Untitled, brooch, fabricated and reticulated, sterling silver and obsidian, 2.5" x 1" x 1.25", 1991.

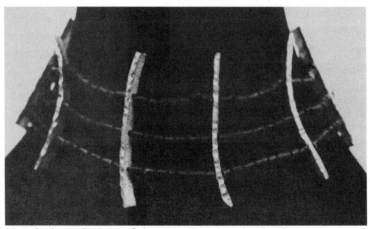

Photo credit:
David LaPlantz

Untitled, neckpiece, fabricated and etched, aluminum and beads, 16" x 1" x 2.25", 1991.

Terri Gelenian-Wood

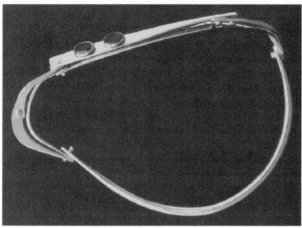

Sikyatki, bracelet, forged and riveted, sterling silver and garnets, 3.5" x 2.25" x .25", 1989.* Copyright 1989 Terri Gelenian-Wood

Landscape Pins, anodized and assembled, aluminum, acrylic and architect's symbols, 3.5" x 1.25" x .25", 1991. Copyright 1991 Terri Gelenian-Wood

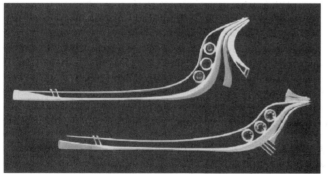

Top: Breath-feather, brooch, sterling and amethysts, 5.25" x 1.75" x .5"; Bottom: Shongopovi, brooch, sterling and peridot, 5.24" x 1" x .25"; Both: forged and riveted, 1989.* Copyright 1989 Terri Gelenian-Wood

*Photo credit: Ralph Gabriner

Metal-Meditation

by Marjorie Simon

Recently I attended a slide lecture given by a colleague in ceramics. I listened to her impassioned talk about her work. Her large hand-built sculptural vessels reveal a raw earthen spirituality. She showed slides of the desert, talked about challenges of scale, and in using imagery all around us. Some of her thoughts I understood instantly as an artist — the notion of looking closely at objects and seeing them in a different

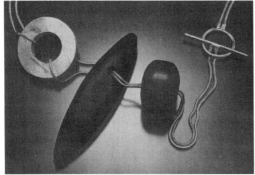

Spheres & Spears Series SAA, fabricated and carved, sterling, acrylic and amber bead: .25" x 2" dia, spear: 3", 1991.

Article photo credit: Ralph Gabriner

scale; as a jeweler I often read free-standing stone sculpture as pins. This was familiar. But this spiritual connection to the land was not in my lexicon. I believed intellectually what she was saying, but it didn't resonate emotionally for me.

What is it about metal that explains my attraction to it? What makes me consider myself a metallist first, even though I work in many alternative materials? The great 19th century sociologist, Max Weber, coined the phrase "elective affinity," originally to describe the correspondence between ideas and their social adherents, such as early capitalism finding fertile roots in Christianity.

Similarly, I believe the choice of a medium for creative expression depends on an affinity between the individual and some intrinsic quality of the medium. The choice is non-rational, and, only after the fact does one explain the attraction. Does anyone care that metalwork began after man had achieved a fairly high level of cultural evolution, about 4,000-6,000 years ago? That technology had advanced beyond forming bits of meteoric minerals to extracting metal from the earth, cleaning, beatify and riveting it? These intellectual connections appear only after the fact, in reflection. Of the two distinguishing characteristics of substances known as the class of metals, only one, that it is shiny, is likely to have an emotional appeal. The other, that it is a good conductor of heat and electricity doesn't carry much emotional weight. Not all metals are equally appealing. The purity of silver attracts by its whiteness, copper by its malleability. Only gold, the most ductile, seduces by its luster and sensuous surface. Later one discovers the immensely appealing characteristic of its polishing up beautifully, despite scratching during fabrication.

Creative people have before them an enormous range of potential materials. What makes someone choose metal over clay, paint over glass, broken car glass, pink marble, or salvaged wood as a primary material? Describing the properties of the medium is not the same as being able to explain the emotional attachment. At the same time, the (creative) idea determines the choice of materials. A metalsmith is not likely to conceive of exploring the duality of interior/exterior in a tapestry; we think of form (fabricated?), texture (etched, roller printed or chased?), and so on, in the context of a hard three-dimensional object whose surface is shiny or matte. I think all artists have a "first love" in terms of medium and I'm concerned about this attraction. Often the attraction or repulsion of a material is quite visceral. A paper maker says she cannot tolerate the scrape of metal against metal. I detest the feel of construction paper on my skin. I don't particularly like being wet; therefore I'll never be a paper maker.

My affinity for metal also involves the human transformation of a natural material. On a recent trip to Alaska I discovered that I was more responsive to spirit masks and carvings of ravens than I was to the ravens themselves. Ultimately what moved me was the transformed image, filtered through human experience and human hands. This reaction is entirely consistent with my urban, people-oriented world-view and my choice of metal as a means of expression. Unlike clay, metal is transformed by human hands and tools before it even gets to me. It's structure, machined and refined, is there; you need only to fold it, strike it, heat it, change it, but the internal structure exists as a promise of things to come. I find clay to possess an intimidating quality because of its infinite malleability (start with mud and make whatever you want). Metal, however, is gratefully lacking in that quality (start with a sheet and see what you can do with it).

New Spheres & Spears Series GC, roller printed, etched and carved, sterling silver, acrylic, vermeil, 14k gold, garnet and rose quartz, bead: 2" dia, spear: 3", 1990-91.

The use of metal for human ornamentation thus becomes a natural expression of several deeply held beliefs. This connection of jewelry and metal may not apply to those who make hollowware or ritual objects. For me the durability of ornamentation remains a factor. Firmly grounded in our culture, metal jewelry is a permanent

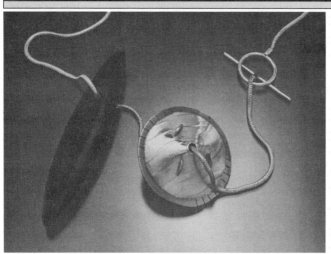
Spheres & Spears Cone Series G, fabricated and carved, sterling, copper and acrylic, bead: 2.4" dia, spear: 3", 1990.

possession of the person wearing it (as opposed to body painting, make-up or other types of ephemeral ornamentation). Again, not a conscious choice, but when a client and friend said to me, "I think of you every day when I get dressed for work," I realized I truly enjoyed being a part of another's life in that way. Jewelry goes right on another person's body. And so it is the connection to people, always primary in my life, that has determined my choice of creative expression. My anthropomorphic imagery found a perfect mate on the human body; it comes to life when worn. Even some "unwearable" jewelry becomes human theater when brought to the body. It is no accident then, that a decision to make jewelry comes to one for whom relationships are crucial. This too, is consistent with a world-view that responds to human creativity over natural wonders.

In exploring these ideas I came on (there are no accidents) an old article by Philip Morton in "Metalsmith" magazine entitled He*phaestus, God of Fire and Metalsmithing.* Among other intriguing interpretations, Morton (once known for his seminal volume on jewelry design and now a practicing psychotherapist) suggests that the femi-

nine unconscious (creativity) plays a part in metalsmithing. He goes on to suggest that, "Hephaestus is a child of the matriarchy rather than the patriarchy." ("Metalsmith," v.3,1, 1983, pp 8-9) Now here is an intriguing idea; first, metalsmithing is gender-neutral. The tools used may compensate for inequality in upper body strength of men and women. Certainly creativity knows no gender, although there seems to be different media in which men and women are over (or under) represented, notably weaving as a traditionally female pursuit and glass-blowing as male. The fact that society has traditionally rewarded male (fine) artists more than female (craft) artists has nothing to do with the nature of creativity itself. Although I hadn't thought of this connection before I rather like the idea that metalworking, not just smithing, does embrace our androgynous nature. The (masculine) urge to control this seemingly unyielding material merges with the (feminine) expressive impulse.

I believe all artists have made these kinds of choices and are aware of them, when they take time to reflect. I offer my ideas as a meditation on a medium. A craftsperson's love of material is reflected in the work. The work of the best metalsmiths reveals the depth of this affection — caressing the surface, teasing the form into life, defying its properties while celebrating them.

copyright 1992 Marjorie Simon

I was trained as a sociologist but I've been an artist all my life. Living near New York enabled me to study with Enid Kaplan and Bob Ebendorf, who nurtured and challenged me. Now I'm a studio jeweler with a particular interest in the Bead; I give workshops in metal and non-metal bead fabrication.

Joann Pedersen Lutz

Confetti and Razor Shell Collection, earrings, embossed and forged, sterling, 14k and 24k keum-bo, 2" x 1": 2.5" x 1.5": 1.25" x .75", 1991. Copyright 1991 Joann Pedersen Lutz

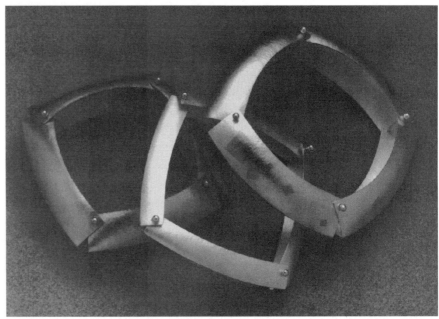

Confetti and Razor Shell Collection, bangle bracelets, embossed and forged, 14k, sterling and 24k keum-bo, 3.25" x 1": 3.25" x .5": 3.5" x 1", 1991. Copyright 1991 Joann Pedersen Lutz

Terry A. Moore

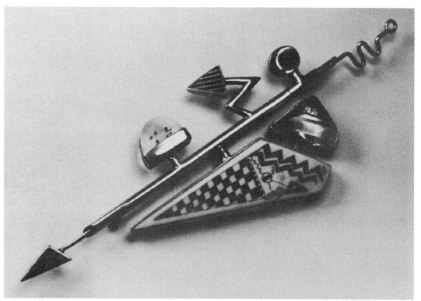

Elvis is Sighted at the Oil Spill, scrimshaw, forged and constructed, silver, 14k, mokume, tourmaline, rutilated quartz and mammoth ivory, 4.5" x 2" x .5", 1992.

Along for the Ride, carved, turned, forged and scrimshaw, mammoth ivory and bone, mokume, and silver, 3" x 1.75", 1991.

Photo credit: Pat Davis Candler

Jennifer Rabe

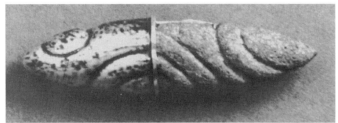

Brooch, repousse, chasing and cast, sterling and cement, 3" x 1" x .5", 1991.

Brooch, carved with inlay, ebony, purple heart and sterling, 3" x 1" x .5", 1991.

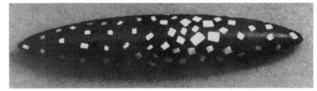

Brooch, enameling, fine silver, 3" x .5", 1991.

Bracelet, fabricated and fold formed, sterling, 1.25" x 1", 1990.

Judith Kinghorn

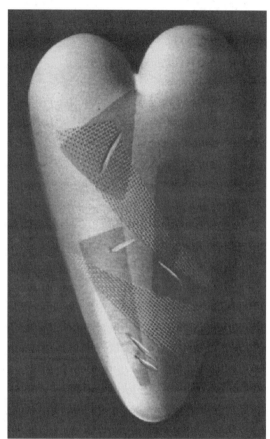

Heat Pin, hollow formed, fused, roller pinted and constructed, 24k gold and sterling silver, 2" x 1.25" x .25", 1992.

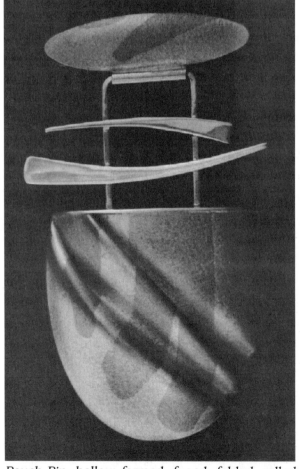

Pouch Pin, hollow formed, fused, folded, rolled printed and constructed, 24k gold and sterling silver, 2.25" x 1.25" x .25", 1992.

Photo credit: Michael Knott

Sheila Satow

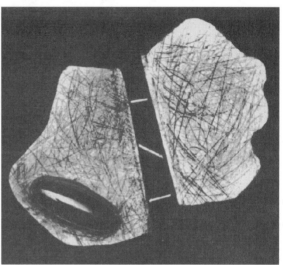

Untitled, fabricated and roller printed, 18k gold, sterling silver, malachite and turquoise, 2.25" x 2.5" x .25", 1992.

Detached Cohesion, fabricated with file texture, sterling and hematite, 1.75" x 2.5" x .5", 1991.

Empower & Rejoice Series, fabricated with file texture, sterling with stones, 2.25" x 1.25" x .25": 1.5" x 1" x .25": 2" x 1.25" x .25", 1991.

Photo credit: Barry Blau

Carol Adams
Florence Resnikoff

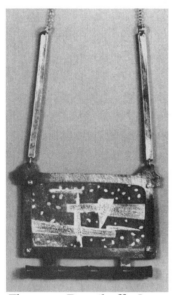

Florence Resnikoff, Japanese Palimpsest, neckpiece, fabricated and fused, 24k and 18k gold, palladium, niobium, and onyx, 11.25" x 2.5", 1990.*

Florence Resnikoff, The Ribbon is the Message, earrings, fabricated, palladium, 14k gold and pearls, 1" x 2.5", 1990.*

*Photo credit: Gary Sinick

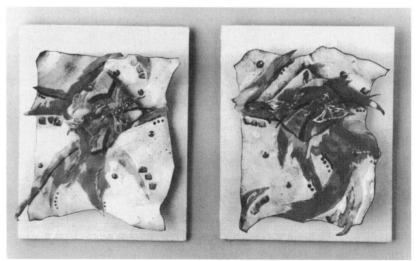

Carol Adams, Haiti III & IV: Winged Creatures, limoges, enamel, felt and stitchery, 4.5" x 15" x 18", 1990. Photo credit: Bruce Gates

Eun-Mee Chung

Why Not Follow Birds?, brooch, fabricated, roll printed and keum-boo, sterling silver, 24k gold and copper, 4" x 2.5" x .25", 1991.

Nothing, neckpiece and brooch, fabricated and roll printed, sterling silver and gold leaf, 2" x 1" x .5", 1992.

A Doll House #1, fabricated, brooch on table sculpture, hydro pressed and keum-boo sterling silver, copper and 24k gold, 10" x 2.5" x 1", 1992.

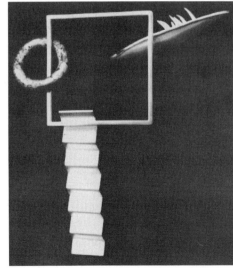

Sitting by the Window, brooch, fabricated, keum-boo and hydro pressed, sterling silver and 24k gold, 4" x 3" x .75", 1992.

Irene Embrey
Beth Piver

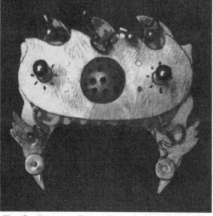

Irene Embrey, Cosas Elementales, Shi-Shi Stones, fabrication, 5" x 2.25", 1992.*

Photo credit: R Embrey

Irene Embrey, Cosas Elementales, Shi-Shi Stones, fabricated, mokume-gane, silver and copper, 3" x 2.25", 1992.*

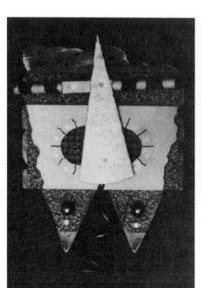

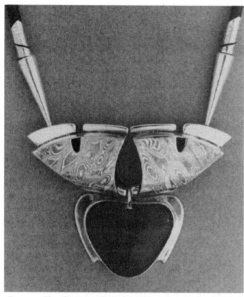

Beth Piver, Sea Creature, brooch, constructed, sterling, niobium and aluminum, 2" x 2.25" x .75", 1991.

Beth Piver, TV, brooch, constructed, copper, sterling, brass, aluminum, wood and Formica, 3" x 2" x .5", 1991.

Beth Piver, Astro Bull, brooch, constructed, cooper, brass, sterling, aluminum, Formica and plastic, 2.5" x 3.5" x .5", 1991.

Machine Pin #2, fabricated, sterling silver, brass, copper and micarta, 3" x 1.5" x .5", 1991.

Hans Ruebel

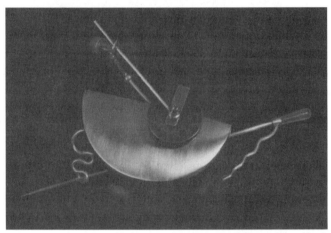

Machine Pin #1, fabricated, cast and forged, nickel, bronze, sterling silver and pink quartz, 6" x 3" x 1.5", 1991.

Machine Pin #3, fabricated and cast, sterling and fine silver, bocote and cocobola, 3.5" x 2" x .25", 1991.

Straight Edge II, damascus and blacksmithing, 01 and mild steel, nickel, sterling and Micarta, 7" x 1" x .5", 1991.

Straight Edge Knife, Damascus and blacksmithing, mild and 01 steel, bocote, nickel and Micarta, 8" x 1" x .5", 1991.

Folding Knives

by Bob Coogan

The folding knife is one of the most common and useful tools. My own interest stems from childhood; I've carried a knife for as long as I can remember and use it every day. When I began to study art and consider questions of form and function it occurred to me that the knife is a perfect blend of design and utility. This article will teach you how to construct your own folding knife, blending aesthetic and practical considerations so that the end result is a unique working tool.

Begin by examining a good folding knife. What pleases you about the design and function? What would you change? Consider the purpose of your own knife. Do you want it to be strong and durable, something that will take a beating on the camping trail, or do you think of it as a sculptural object? Is it to cut meat, take on a picnic, carve wood, or wear around your neck?

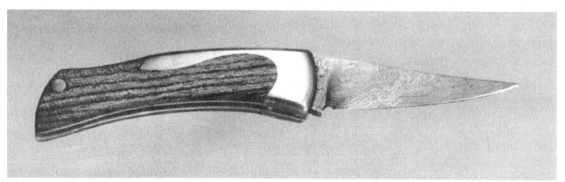

Picket Knife, forged and fabricated, Damascus steel, brass and rosewood, 5" x .5" x .5", 1990.

As you examine the knife before you, notice that the blade stays locked in position when closed, flows smoothly to a 90° angle, then hesitates. This is a safety device to keep it from closing on your fingers. When fully open the blade snaps into position with the spring holding it. When closed, the knife rests with the cutting edge completely concealed. This 2-step operation is referred to as the "walk and talk" of the knife. Of course the best way to understand how the knife works is to take it apart, examine the way the parts interact, and then reassemble it.

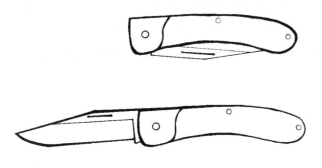

Designing

Begin by drawing your knife on paper; draw it with the blade both open and closed. To be sure that the blade with fit into the handle: make a paper cutout of the blade, place a pin through the pivot hole and then swivel the blade to a closed position. The relationship of all parts is essential to the harmony of the whole. So, examine the design to see if it works with your original goals; if you are satisfied begin to make the interior drawings.

Once again you must consider the knife both open and closed. First design the tang end of the blade. Since most of the stress is taken by the tang, it's critical that this is laid out properly. If not, the knife won't "walk and talk" smoothly. Draw the back square, where the spring rests when the blade is in the open position. Next draw the tang front, including the kick; this is where

Detail of Tang

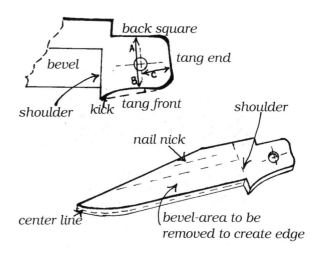

the spring rests with the blade in the closed position. Then, determine the location of the 1/8" diameter pivot hole; it should be centered half-way between the back square and tang front, slightly further in from the tang end. The tang end should have a flat spot in its center to form a safety stop. The corners should be round enough to allow for smooth operation yet abrupt enough to enable the blade to snap into position. Make sure that when closed the kick and the tang end are in contact with the spring, but, the cutting edge is not touching. The spring should be flush with the back of the handle, whether the blade is open or closed. This is accomplished by designing the spring without the blade in position. It should have a slight curve form the midpoint to the tip and rest close to the pivot hole. This assures the blade with be under constant tension.

Each person must decide for themselves how safety conscious they will be. This article shows one artist's approach to their own studio work. Do not follow it verbatim -- decide for yourself on the important issues of health and safety. See page 3.

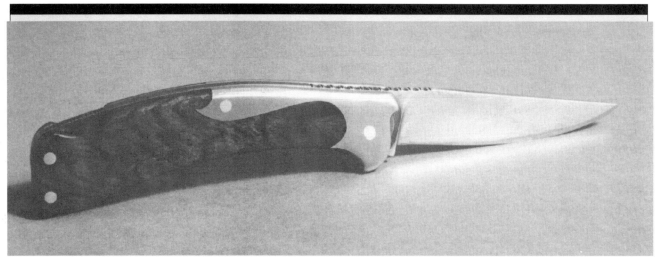

Kenya Folder, a lock blade folder, fabricated, 01 tool steel, brass and rosewood, 7.5" x .5" x 1.5", 1989.

Internal Structure

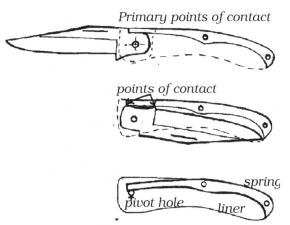

Primary points of contact

points of contact

spring

pivot hole *liner*

The spring should be designed like this to insure proper tension on blade.

Exploded View

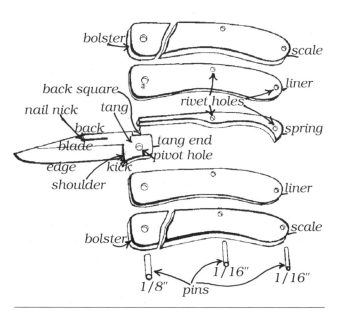

bolster *scale*

liner

back square
rivet holes
nail nick *tang*
back *spring*
blade *tang end*
edge *pivot hole*
kick
shoulder *liner*

bolster *scale*

1/16" *1/16"*
1/8" *pins*

The spring is held in place with two pins (1/16" dia.) one at the end farthest from the blade and one in the middle. The area from the middle pin to the blade should be of uniform thickness allowing even flexion over the entire length. If the spring is too tight after tempering, metal can be removed from the inside edge in order to increase flexibility.

At the same time that the blade and spring are laid out, draw the lines, bolsters and scales. The liners cover the inside handle of the knife, the shape of the back is the same as the outside edge of the spring. They must be long enough to contain both the closed blade and spring and narrow enough to enable you to grasp the blade. The bolster is a solid piece of metal that acts as a support structure for the blade and pivot pin; it defines the blade end of the handle. The 1/8" pivot pin connects the bolster and the blade. The scales are usually wood or plastic and cover the liners with the bolsters joining them at one end.

Making the Knife

To make your own knife I recommend the following materials:

1. 6" x 1/8" x 1" — 01 tool steel for blade and spring (01 is easily obtainable and can be worked with hand tools or simple machines).

2. 18 gauge brass for lines, 1/8" brass for bolsters.

3. 1/8" and 1/16" brass rods for pins.

4. Any good hardwood for the scales. These materials can vary, depending on your design.

I like to make paper patterns of all components and transfer the to steel using a permanent marking pen. Mark all the holes to be drilled with a center punch an drill them with a drill press, making sure that the holes are straight and that they match the pins perfectly. Be sure to do this before cutting the pieces, since it's easier and safer to hold a larger piece of steel. Now, using a jeweler's saw, a steel cutting band saw or a hack saw, (a good hack saw with a bi-metal blade is fast and last a long time) begin cutting out the pieces then refine the profiles by filing and sanding the edges with 220 grit sandpaper. The next step is to layout the taper on the flat side of the blade. Start by drawing a center line down the length of the cutting edge and lay out the shoulders carefully matching them on both sides. The actual taper starts about 3/4 of the distance from the cutting edge to the back, although this varies from knife to knife. Clamp the blade flat to a table and file off the steel from the line near the back and the shoulder to the edge; then flip it over and do the other side making sure the shoulders and the to line match on both sides. Refine by sanding with 220. The last detail is the nail nick, the thin groove you catch with your fingernail in order to open the knife. This I simply grind in with either a separating disk or a grinding burr on the flexible shaft.

Now lay out two liners and two bolsters, connecting the uncut pieces of brass with Super Glue. Drill the two 1/16" holes in the liners using th e spring as a guide and drill the 1/8" hole for the pivot pin last. Be sure to insert a pin after each hole to insure there will be no slippage. Drill the bolsters with a 1/8" hole. Cut to shape. File all contours until smooth. Once you have refined the profiles pull the bolsters and liners apart. Clean the surfaces (the Super Glue bond can be broken by heating to about 350°) then, using silver solder, solder the bolsters to the liners.

Hardening and Tempering

If you buy a full length of 01 tool steel (36") it will come with heat treating instructions. Heat treating is actually a two stage process that begins with hardening. This changes the molecular structure of the steel, making it hard and brittle. To harden, we need a torch and about 1/2 gallon of quenching oil (a good quality vegetable oil, olive oil or very light motor oil will do). Using the torch, heat the blade to a dull red color, about 1450°F, then plunge it into the oil. Quench for about one minute. Then the blade will be cool enough to remove from the oil and set aside. Repeat this process with the spring. When cool enough to handle, was the oil from the blade and spring and sand both parts back to bare metal.

Now it's time for tempering, a balancing act that will eliminate the brittleness caused by hardening while retaining the strength and edge holding ability of the steel. The easiest way to temper is in a kiln or oven, the blade should be heated to 450° for an hour and then removed to air temperature to cool. The spring should be heated to 600° for an hour. If this intensity of heat is impossible, tempering can be done with a torch, although the technique is tricky and may require some practice. As the steel is heated it progresses through a rainbow of colors, each one indicating a specific temperature. First it's straw yellow, then purple and blue, finally changing to a silver gray. For the cutting edge we don't want to pass straw yellow and for the spring a rich blue. Holding the tang with pliers or tongs, heat the blade gently from the back along the entire length. The colors will gradually appear and begin to move downward. The trick is to pull the torch away so that the straw yellow stops at the cutting edge. Hold the spring in a similar fashion, heating it past the straw color and stopping at blue. If either piece is overheated you will have to re-harden and temper again. When the tempering is correct, smooth and polish all parts.

Finishing

Final refining of the sides will take place after initial assembly and the wood can be fitted at this time. To achieve a perfect fit shape only the ends (of the wood) that will come in contact with the bolsters and then epoxy the wood in place. After the glue dries the wood can be drilled through the existing holes and the contours can be evened.

To assemble, I place a pin in the hole farthest from the blade, going through each side of the knife and through the spring in the center. Next I place the pivot pin through both bolsters, piercing the blade. The trick now is to get the pin in the middle hole. The best way to do this is to place the knife on its side, blade open, in a vice (like a Panavice) with soft jaws touching the spring on one side and the liners on The other. By gently tightening the vice the spring should come into line so that the pin can be dropped into place. If it won't line up you may have to remove a small amount of steel from the blade end of the spring; if the spring is too short you will need to make

another. I taper one end of each pin in order to make alignment easier.

Once you've assembled the knife, examine how all the parts work together. The back spring and blade should have a nice straight line; the blade should flow smoothly and freely with the spring under constant tension. If it all works well, take your knife apart, refine and polish all the parts and countersink the holes, then assemble and set the rivets with a hammer. In order to insure that the pivot pin isn't too tight I slide a very thin piece of steel shim stock between the blade and liner then remove it after the rivet is set. Finally, polish the exterior surface, place a drop of light machine oil on the hinge, sharpen the knife and it's finished.

Now, examine your work to see if it fulfills your original goals. Use your knife and get to know it. Does it feel good in your hand? Is it balanced? Does the blade do what you want it to? Does the form please your eye? Making a working tool that is also a thing of beauty is very satisfying and the knowledge gained through the process can be applied to other things. Use your experience with this knife as a starting point, learn from it and go on to explore new ideas.

Robert Coogan grew up in California, completed his MFA at Cranbrook Academy of Art and spent a year teaching in England on a Fulbright Exchange Program. He has been head of the Metals Department at the Appalachian Center for Crafts in Smithville, TN for the last eleven years. Bob is equally at home creating fine jewelry, hollowware or hammering away in the Smithy. He has taught workshops nationally an internationally and is known for his beautifully designed knives and his work in Damascus steel.

Gretchen Krutz
Tom Shurr

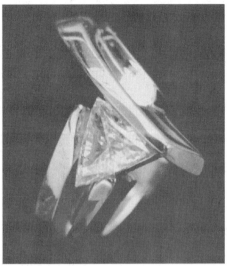

Gretchen Krutz, ring, cast, 14k gold, 1990.

Tom Shurr, Untitled, pin, cast and forged, fine and sterling silver, 14k gold and cocobolo, 4" x 1.5" x .5".

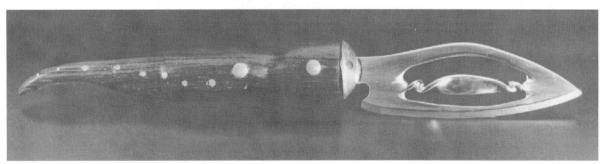

Tom Shurr, knife, forged, stainless steel, cocobolo and brass, 9.5" x 2.5" x 1.5", 1991. Photo credit: Brian Huntley

Joan Dulla
Amy Mertus

Amy Mertus, In Full Bloom, chased and repousse, and cast, sterling silver and bronze, 6" x 4" x 3", 1991. Photo credit: Brian Huntley

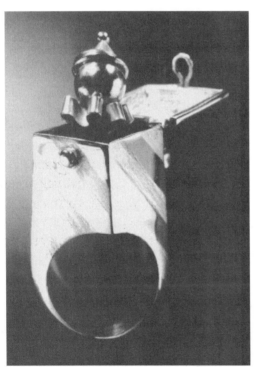

Joan Dulla, Jock-In-A-Box, fabrication, silver and 14k gold, 2" x 2" x 2", 1990.*

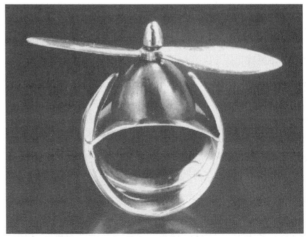

Joan Dulla, Propeller, fabrication, silver and mokume-gane, 1" x 1" x 1", 1990.*

*Photo credit: Jeff Scoville

Who's In Charge Anyway?

by David LaPlantz

My theory of life is that <u>no one</u> has the right (or obligation) to give me permission — except me. Yet many of us feel a strong need for others to give us permission, even in the most basic decision making.

Permission Required?

Permission is a requirement for daily living and seems to come two ways; inner and outer. There are the decisions/permission that come from each individual - and then those that come from others, like parents, spouses, teachers, fellow artists, the government, or, simply the ubiquitous "they." Some think, "If I let someone else decide for me, then everything will be okay. Besides, if the decision is incorrect, then it's not my fault. I can blame it on them." Truly a convenient way out.

Certain hours each day are known as "Happy Hour." This is a time when human beings are given permission to be happy. To fulfill this permission we assemble, mix, drink, flirt, act silly, get rowdy and possibly get sick. This is granted to us as a prize, a reward for working hard, being good, whatever. What's next, stars on the calendar?

I don't need anyone telling me when I can be happy. Besides, drinking is not a reward for doing anything, in my opinion. It is up to me to be happy whenever I want to be happy. But if logic rules and we let other's grant us a Happy Hour, then do they also grant an "Unhappy Hour?"

Permission Granted

The trademarked products called Glad Bags have an ingenious yellow and blue zipper-connection which becomes green when the bag is sealed correctly. Is it a coincidence that green is also the street light color meaning "go?" Permission.

Recently I have permitted myself to use any and all materials and techniques. I use whatever will solve a particular artistic situation. Although I've always felt comfortable using materials and techniques as needed, this new level of permission has given me a renewed attitude about making art. I'm thrilled, invigorated and freed. It was as if a wave of new, fresh air blew through my creative spirit and released long dormant creative brain cells.

Realizations?

As a young art student I had two exciting experiences one day, perhaps you can relate. I had been working on a sculpture and felt incredibly close to the piece. I was no longer in the studio working with 25 other people, but all alone within, almost the molecular structure, of the Styrofoam. I felt like I could walk all over the surface, like a character from *Honey, I Shrank the Kids!* The feeling was so powerful I had to share it with my teacher (who was also one of my mentors). His reaction was to tell me how weird I was and that this was one of the silliest things he had ever heard.

I felt a great sense of sorrow for him and jubilation for me. I had just experienced something unique and special! I hoped for similar experiences in the future. (And fortunately I have felt the magic many, many times since.)

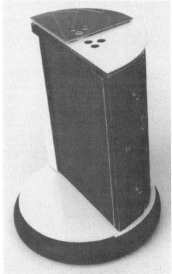

1/4 Of 1/2 Of A Cup, Fabricated, aluminum, wood, contact paper, engraved, 5" x 4.5" dia., 1992.

That particular day was special to me for three reasons:

1. I had experienced something unique and no one could convince me otherwise.

2. I felt sorry for my teacher, he was missing the time of his life and didn't even know it.

3. I began granting permission to David to listen, understand, learn and to disagree. From then on I have worked hard to think for myself, without being clouded and influenced by others, even a respected friend and mentor. He was entitled to his opinions. And so was I.

Some Questions

Do you make your style of art to be hip. Do you employ the technique(s) to be hip or accepted? Are you missing your creative and personal boat while coat-tailing or hitching a ride on (in) someone else's boat (technique/process)? If so, is this the type of permission you're seeking? If you can't think for yourself, why are you making art? Perhaps it would be better to get a job with someone who will tell you exactly what to do every minute of your work day. True, making your own decisions is risky, but therein lies the challenge and joy of being truly creative and in charge of your life and destiny. It's all up to you.

If you disagree, then others decide for you. You are seeking permission from the outside to do everything in your life. A sad commentary on the uniqueness and special gifts inside your creative spirit.

Do you seek permission to do what you really want to do (and know that you can do it), but still need the personal or artistic validation from others?

Is your journey, or goal, the direction you're heading toward, or, has your life's goal become getting validation and permission granted from others?

If I allow others to dictate who I am, I've missed my life's script. Life's script is to discover who we are inside — with whatever magical talents we've been given and can develop from within/without.

Otherwise, if we wait for others to provide the permission we loose precious time, energy and the skills lying just below the surface of our psyche.

Role Model

We are all fans of someone or some cause. The people we most respect create permission granting situations. This happens through what they do, the way they act, the clothes they wear, etc. We, in turn, give them permission to do more by emu-

Slant Cup, fabricated aluminum, contact paper, bronze, cardboard, 8" x 4" x 4", 1992.

lating them. The cycle continues. Think back to when you were younger. Do you recall a certain individual who you respected? Did you dress, walk or talk in a similar way? Do you realize that you are a role model for someone right now? Each of us unknowingly plays that important role to people we will never actually meet. Scary isn't it? Our art is seen by thousands of people and slowly, quietly our artistic vision is opening the minds and hearts of others. What a wonderful way to share the essence of our human spirit!

Permission Granted to David

In the last few months, having allowed myself this new sense of permission, I have seen my art grow and expand into areas I may have secretly wished for in the past. I feel free enough to try any material other than metal, in any size and on any topic or imagery. The old David was often afraid to venture into certain areas of thought or materials because of what I thought others would think. How silly! Who cares what others think? We all do. We would like to be recognized, sell well in galleries, etc.

Now I'm ready to tackle anything coming down the creative freeway. I've even decided to work under a new name. This new persona is called C.O.D. Cheekz. He can do many things I can't. Who knows what I'll learn from him. The new will help improve the old. Isn't life, permission and taking charge of one's actions, great? Freedom, that's what it's all about.

David LaPlantz grew up in a small town in NW Ohio. After graduating from Bowling Green State Univ he moved on to Cranbrook Academy of Art and received his M.F.A. in 1969. He currently teaches Jewelry and Metalsmithing at Humboldt State Univ in Arcata, CA. He authored <u>Artists Anodizing Aluminum: The Sulphuric Acid Process.</u>

Computer Disk Book fabricated, aluminum, contact paper, string and tape, 7" x 7" x 1", 1992.

Thelma Coles Sally-Heath Lloyd

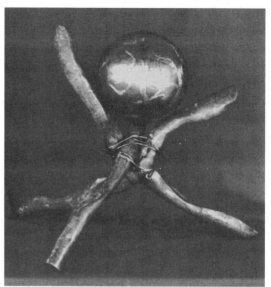

Flora Memories, raised, fabricated, etched and patinated, copper, 20" x 24.5" x 20.5", 1992.

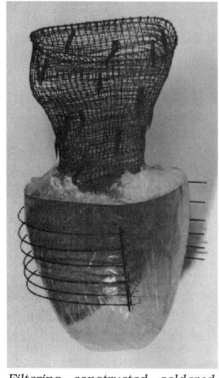

Filtering, constructed, soldered, pressed and twinned, copper, brass, magnet wire, stainless, rice paper, Plexiglas and paint, 14" x 12.5" x 31", 1991.

Boundaries, constructed, soldered and twinned, magnet wire, stainless, rice paper and paint, 20" x 31" x 26", 1990.

Photo credit: Sandy Wilson

182

Elizabeth Barick Fall

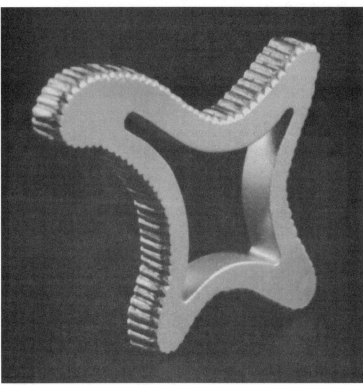

Untitled, ring, married metals and hollow formed, sterling silver, copper and brass, 1.5" x .25" x 1.5", 1992.

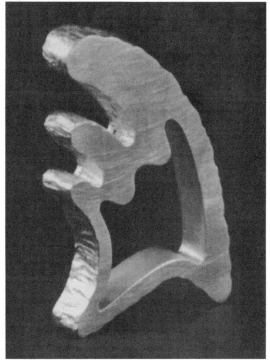

Untitled, ring, hollow formed and reticulated, sterling silver, 1" x .25" x 2", 1992.

Susan E. Sarantos
Edith Sommer

Edith Sommer, Arrows & Ripples, brooch, reticulated and fabricated, sterling, 14k gold, diamond and rose quartz, 2.5" x 2.5", 1990.

Susan E. Sarantos, earrings, fabricated, 18k, orange speckle druse ovals, diamonds and blue chrysocolla druse, .5" x 1.5", 1990.

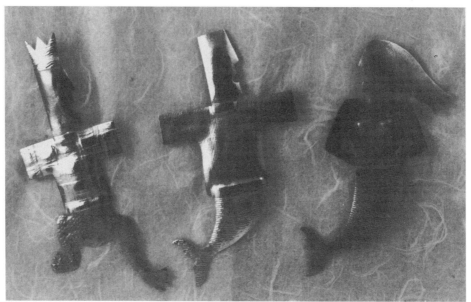

Susan E. Sarantos, Mythical Folk Creatures, fabricated and roll printed, sterling and gold filled copper, ea: 2.25" x 3.5", 1989.

Snaring The Muse

Photo credit: Dennis Heekins

by Elaine Heyman

The Muse has flown! I enter the studio, overwhelmed by an empty feeling. Hoping activity will oil the rusty hinges of my brain, I oil the rusty hinges of my tools. When the work is finished — each tool cleaned and in its place, the floor swept, the entire room tidy — the waiting studio seems to demand, "Well?"

With a growing sense of anxiety at the increasingly empty feeling, I fear that all may be lost. The sensation of pure joy and excitement that accompanies the creative process may never more be mine.

Over the years, I have tried to develop measures to search out the Muse and to snare her yet again. Looking at photographs and illustrations of the work of others does not have an immediately gratifying effect, though this exercise may prove helpful to some. A form of doodling, using non-objective or non-recognizable forms until a clearly defined design emerges, may work for others. However, I have had to look for sources of creativity within myself.

Using my senses of sight and hearing, I open myself to actively seeking, accepting and welcoming ideas. Ideas at whatever moment they appear. Setting problems to be solved seems to arouse a creative response. Seemingly unrelated situations stir new ideas. Walking along the sea wall, seeing the movement of the waves can evoke my attempt to mirror that fluidity in metal.

Listening to "The Babbitt and the Bromide" made me aware of clichés that led to ISN'T IT A S-M-A-L-L WORLD? translated into jewelry. The earwraps depict a sun, moon,

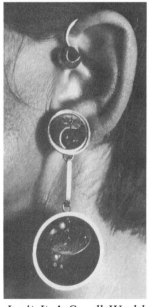

Isn't It A Small World, fabricated, sterling, 4.75" x 1.25" x .5", 1986. © 1986 Elaine Heyman Photo credit: Dennis Heekin

yin and yang symbols, a planet, a galaxy — cupped within dark blue concave semicircles enclosing stars — tiny universes. Of course, the other cliché *IT'S MUSIC TO MY EARS* has been particularly appropriate for concerts. I have met fellow music lovers who used a comment about these ear wraps as an opening gambit for further conversation.

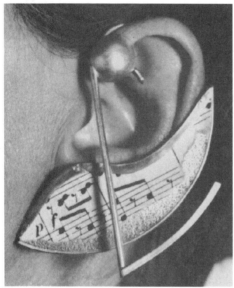

It's Music To My Ears, fabricated and forged, silver, copper and paper, 3" x 1.25" x .75", 1986. Copyright 1986 Elaine Heyman

Sometimes problem solving helps to create new ideas. My inability to tolerate wearing earrings combined with my vanity led me to devise the earwraps. Which in turn allowed me to experiment with different forms of earwraps; covering the ear, dangling, or graceful ribbons of silver outlining the ear.

When I misplaced my pillbox for the thousandth time, my exasperated husband said, "You ought to wear it." Eureka! What a wonderful idea. I could design different types of pillboxes to hang in different ways. Should the neck only be involved or should more of the body support the box? What shapes would efficiently and attractively carry pills? What could be worn for casual dress? What would look better

for more formal occasions? The opportunities and permutations became fun to contemplate and the Muse was cooperative.

Pillbox and Chain, fabricated and forged, sterling and lapis, 4.25" x 2.25" x 1.5", 1985.

A statement with political or emotional overtones can provoke a creative response. When once again I heard Eve blamed for the woes of the world. As a woman I responded with frustration and anger. This anger sparked a *TRIBUTE TO EVE* series of pendants, celebrating her gift of knowledge to the world. They depict *BEGINNING KNOWLEDGE, KNOWLEDGE OF THE PAST, CURRENT KNOWLEDGE,* and *KNOWLEDGE OF THE FUTURE.* An individual who saw a pendant of Eve, the apple and the snake imagery, turned to her companion and said, "Adam I wish you would stop blaming ME — you were the one who was hungry."

Creativity is not limited to one medium or one way of working. It requires a stretching of mind and skills — the appreciation of risk to challenge those skills. Deliberately setting a problem that requires learning a new technique or the use of a new tool or arbitrarily stipulating limits, helps when

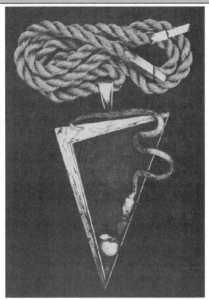

Homage to Eve - Current Knowledge, cast, fabricated and painted, sterling, Color Core and acrylic paint, 5.25" x 3" x 1.5", 1992. Photo credit: Susan Hoisington

I encounter a dry spell.

Setting a task of learning to use the hydraulic press, for example, I developed a "project," limiting myself to geometric forms, in strips of plastic dies that could be interchanged. The goal was to create a strong three-dimensional form, countering the thin gauged silver using the press. The very act of developing this project served to release me from the "blankness" I was experiencing. The result was *URBAN MAGIC* — a necklace and pendant.

By using these projects as a means of risking to learn, the pieces themselves are not pre-planned. They grow and develop as the work progresses and as I open myself to the risk of failure. This is a valuable challenge. If one doesn't risk failure, the alternative is a rehash of past successes.

I have found the creative process to be extremely complex. It is beyond my ability to adequately map the pathways. The creative acts going on unknown to me, even while I am engaged in other disparate occupations; such as gardening, cleaning, listening to music, attending meetings (my attention wanders), painting furniture, etc. Creation in one medium seems to nurture creativity in other mediums. While one part of my mind is occupied with the task at hand, another part is visualizing, discarding and experimenting with all sorts of possibilities.

The constant pressure of unconscious and conscious waiting and thinking continues to build. An almost physical discomfort wells up that cannot be relieved until the creative urge is recognized, the work then progresses on the creative idea that "suddenly" arose. Finally the pleasure, fun and hard work begins.

Sitting beside a pond on his property near his studio, Sandro Chia and I were speaking of dry spells. He said, "All the work, in a sense, is a kind of putting nets to fish," (gesturing to the pond). "The special fish...you don't know what you are going to catch. The only strategy possible is to sink your bait in the darkness of the water and wait, wait for a signal, an indication, a symbol...Lots of times I feel like I am...really empty and banal in a sense. But I need what I think — it's a good exercise...I'm not continuous — I'm not a constant person. The only constant in my life is my work. My work is the big trap that I am building to catch beauty."

So I continue to bait my line, cast it into the waters, and sometimes I am lucky to strike a vibrant, bright, shimmering idea — to be caught and transformed into a moment of beauty in precious metal.

Retiring from varied careers (graphic artist, newspaper editor, psychotherapist, department head and tenured faculty of a medical school), I turned to metalsmithing. Lucky in my choice of teachers — Rolf Scarlett (avant-garde at age 90), Bob Ebendorf, Jamie Bennett and Lynda Watson-Abbott, I continue to seek challenges by creating one-of-a-kind jewelry.

Carla J. Polek

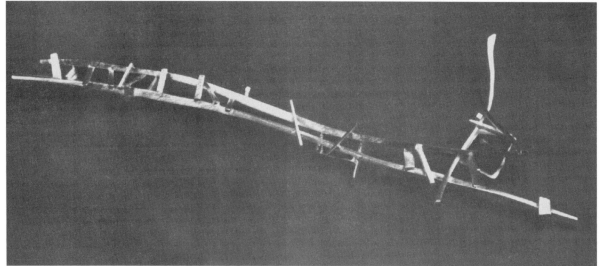

The Relinquished Episode, forged and fabricated, silver and found object, 5.75" x 2.25", 1991.

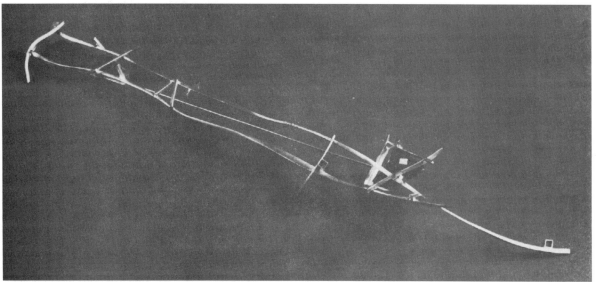

Night Time Companion, forged and fabricated, silver and found object, 10.25" x 1.25", 1991.

Photo credit: Dan Kenner

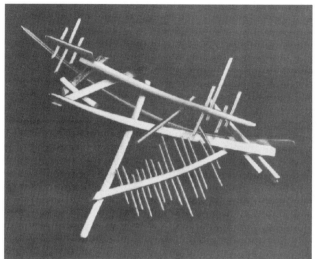

Em Passant, constructed, sterling silver, 3" x .5" x 2.5", 1992.

Theresa Lovering-Brown

Conveyance, constructed, sterling silver and bronze, 6" x 2" x 1", 1991.

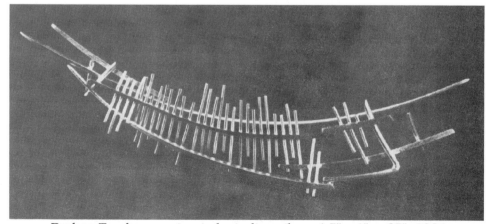

Broken Tracks, constructed, sterling silver, 4.5" x 1" x .25", 1991

Photo credit:
Dan Kenner Photography

Micki Lippe
Jane Martin

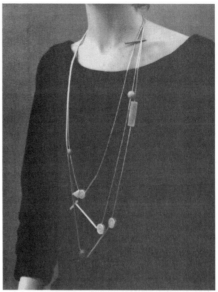

Micki Lippe, Orbit Neckpieces, roll printed and fabricated, sterling silver, 22k gold, copper and turquoise, 1992.*

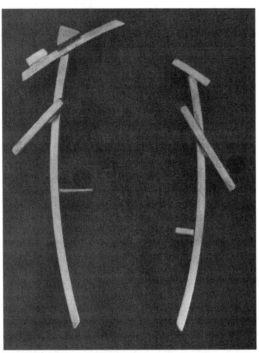

Micki Lippe, This 'n That Earrings, fabricated, sterling, 22k gold and onyx, 2.5", 1992.*

Jane Martin, Chaos Necklace and Earrings, constructed, sterling silver, brass, copper, nickel, agate and jasper, N: 30", E: 1.75" dia., 1991. Photo credit: Roger Schreiber

*Photo credit: Richard Nicol

Nancy Piccioni

Keum-boo Choker, keum-boo, die formed and hollow constructed, sterling silver, and 24k gold, beads: 1", 1990.

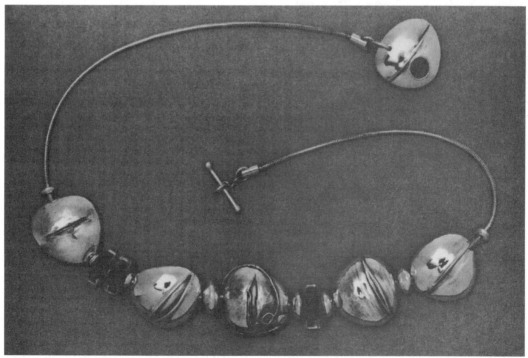

Folded Bead Necklace, folded, die formed, fused and hollow constructed, sterling silver and hand blow glass beads, S/S beads: 1", 1990.

Photo credit: Paul Neevel

Thomas R. Kemerly

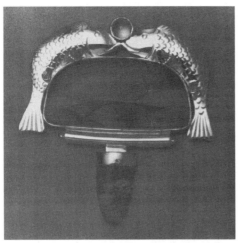

Fish Tales, brooch, fabricated, sterling silver, 14k gold, jasper, rutilated quartz and topaz, 2.25″ x 2″ x .25″, 1992.

Shaman's Anatomy, necklace, fabricated, sterling silver, jasper, topaz, citrine and silk, 4.5″ x 1.5″ x .5″, 1991.

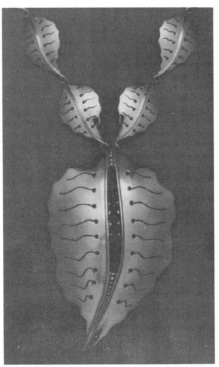

Leaf Necklace, fabricated, sterling silver and garnet, 12″ x 2.25″ x .25″, 1991.

Squid, fabricated and forged, sterling silver, psilomolene tourmaline and silk, 5.5″ x 2.25″ x .5″, 1991.

Photo credit: Kevin Montague

Oxide Enamel Painting

by Yoshiko Yamamoto

I am a self-taught enamelist. I first experimented with enamels in the early seventies. By chance, I found a book, The Enamelist by Kenneth F. Bates, which was the only hands-on book then. I began to work. My early enamel work was mostly playing with transparent colors and cloisonné wire on 18 gauge fine silver.

In 1989 I participated in the *Summer 6 Program* (a one week enamel workshop) at Skidmore College. Jamie Bennett was the instructor. One of the many techniques I learned was oxide enamel painting. This opened up new horizons for my work. The oxide enamels are pigments of mineral compounds and also metal oxides. These finely powdered pigments are mixed with "Thinning oil A-5" (produced from pine oil)* and applied with a brush to the already enameled base. The base's surface must be roughened either by stoning, sandblasting or etching (320 or 400 grit emery paper works as well). The beauty of oxide enamel painting is a free-hand application: either a spontaneous painterly effect or a controlled design can be done. Also, this process can be layered on a regularly enameled surface, (i.e. like a sandwich).

The first firing after the oxide painting application is at 1100°F (don't over fire!). Then when it's cooled, the surface is thinly coated with clear flux 1209 (now 2020) and refired at 1500°F. At this point, sometimes color changes occur. Particularly, red, orange and yellow tend to turn brownish.

I have been experimenting with this fascinating process since I first tried it. Sometimes with a bit of frustration because it's quite difficult to achieve the colors expected.

Recently the opportunity arrived to study at Fachhochschule fur Gestaltung in Pforzheim, Germany during the spring of 1991. A grant from the Mellon Foundation enabled me to go there to research oxide enameling. Why FHG? I didn't have much information about other schools offering the oxide enamel technique. I had also traveled to West Germany the previous year, including a visit to Pforzheim Schmuckmuseum and FHG. I had seen some interesting enameling works from that school. Susanne Miller was an enameling instructor there. Plus, the school has many samples from the past, 1940 to current work.

I learned two different working methods of oxide enameling there. My lack of German and Susanne's lack of English was the only obstacle between us. But we could communicate with each other with body and sign language. I was fortunate to encounter Prof. Dill who was a bilingualist. No wonder, he was originally from the Black Forest, an Alumna of FHG, and now teaching in the Creative Art Program at University Stellgy Bosch in South Africa. He was on a sabbatical leave and revisiting FHG researching enamel work as well. So, we were a good team and shared the information.

Here are two methods of oxide enamel paintings:
1. Using regular gum-binding
2. Using thinning oil.

Each person must decide for themselves how safety conscious they will be. This article shows one artist's approach to their own studio work. Do not follow it verbatim -- decide for yourself on the important issues of health and safety. See page 3.

Using Regular Gum-binding

This process was a revolutionary idea for me. Without using "thinning oil" it's a much simpler process; no surface matting, no rinsing brushes each time with alcohol, shorter drying time, etc.

We can use regular gum-binding, such as Klyr-fire, gum tragacanth, or CMC (a synthetic gum arabic, Carboxy Methyl Cellulose). They are agents commonly used in enameling to hold enamel grits to the base surface. Klyr-fire and gum tragacanth are all from organic gum products like sea-weed, methyl-ethyl-cellulose. They are all water soluble gum-bindings. We did not matte the surface before applying the oxide colors. Of course we could work on a matte surface. We simply mixed the oxide colors with binding agent and applied it with a brush or pen on the prepared base-coated piece and let the binding agent (gum) dry. Then fired it at a normal temperature of 850°C (1500°F). Clear flux can be coated in between the firing, but it's not necessary. I could stone the piece, reapply more colors, and refire it until I reached a satisfactory point.

Using Thinning Oil

The oil mixing method was similar to what I learned at Skidmore. Turpentine was used for rinsing the oiled brush. Again, paint on a smooth surface with a brush or a pen. In this case, after a painting is done, the piece should be dried for at least one hour. Then before firing, the piece is put into the kiln with a fork for a second or two to test if it's completely dried or not. If no smoke comes out from the piece, it can be fired at a normal temperature. If black smoke comes out from the piece, it means the oil is not dried yet and should not be fired.

The school has temperature controlled kilns. As the temperature is set, the students are free from concern about loosing the heat of the kiln or the temperature getting too high when the kiln is not in use.

In both methods they use a white under coat as a base color. But I think we can use any light color as a base.

Since I came back from Germany, I've tried the same processes using Thompson's oxide colors, Klyr-fire and CMC. They worked just as well. I'm still not always achieving the right colors effectively, but I can work much quicker now, using the gum-bindings almost exclusively.

My recent conversation with Tom Ellis, the editor of "Glass on Metal," was extremely helpful. He said that A-5 will give a characteristic color better than using gum-bindings. He also mentioned that using "painting flux" with red, orange or yellow will help to bring the colors out more satisfactorily.

Some of you may already have known about this information, but for em this was an exciting new experience. I thought I would share the information with you in case you haven't tried these techniques yet.

*from a conversation with Tom Ellis

I have encountered two remarkable people in my life. One who encouraged me to set off for Boston more than twenty years ago. The other was the late Miye Matsukata, artist-goldsmith and one of the founding members of SNAG, whom I worked with for nearly eight years. She possessed a marvelous personality, dignity and great imagination. She profoundly influenced my life.

Neckpiece: 18k gold and aquamarine crystal, Brooch: 18k and 24k gold and tourmaline, Earrings: 18k and 22k gold, south sea pearls and ruby.

Deborah Lozier

Shield Pendant with Lace Forehead, hollow formed, copper, silver, brass and enamel, 3" x 1.5", 15", 1991.

Dancing Arch Pendant, hollow formed, copper, silver, brass, enamel and reflectors, 3.5" x .75" x 13", 1991.

Half Moon Pendant, hollow formed, copper, silver, brass and enamel, 2.25" x .75" x 15", 1990.

Nancy J. Young

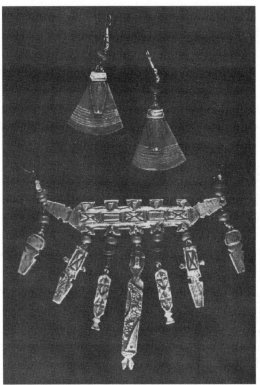

Spirit Guide Necklace #2,
bronze, leather and beads, 8"
x 3" x .5", 1991.

Spirit Guide Necklace, bronze, leather and
beads, 8" x 5" x .5", 1991.

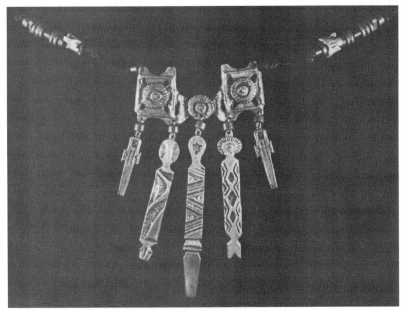

Spirit Guide Necklace #4, bronze, leather and beads, 8" x 3.5" x
.5", 1991.

Rob Milton

Thinking of Leah, fabricated, etched and pierced, mild steel, nickel, copper and garnet, 5" x 5", 1991.

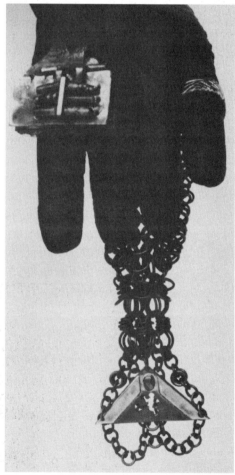

Truckin' (Thinking of Uncle Bob), fabricated and pierced, fine silver, bronze, mild steel, copper, brass, nickel and malachite, 7.5" x 2", 1992.

Photo credit: David LaPlantz

Wanda Bjerke

Untitled, chain mail and repousse, sterling silver and glass stones, 7.5" x 6" x 2", 1988.

Feline Fantasy, chain mail and repousse, sterling silver, tourmalines and citrines, 16" x 10" x 2.5", 1989. Photo credit: GF Photo

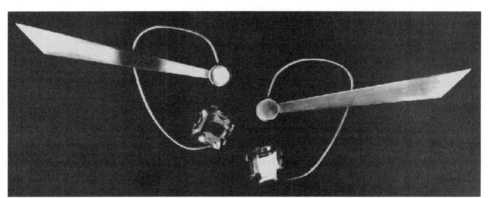

Star Trek 2000, sterling silver and glass stones, 3.5" x 2.5", 1989. (Ear covers that hold the hair back.)

Linda Kaye-Moses

Raphaella Pin, cast, die formed and engraved, sterling silver and semi-precious beads, 1991.

Love's Old Sweet Song, neckpiece, die formed and engraved, sterling silver, 14k gold, amethyst, opal, aquamarine and tourmaline, 3.5" x 2.5", 1991.

Etruria I, fibula, die formed and engraved, sterling silver, 14k gold and iolite, 3" x 3", 1991.

Secrets, neckpiece, die formed, fold formed and engraved, sterling silver, 14k gold, citrine, lapis, turquoise, quartz, gambling token and Favrile glass, 27", 1991.

Photo credit: Evan Soldinger

Rhonda Shikanai

This Happens in March, fabricated, sterling silver, blue topaz and boulder opal, 5.5" x 2" x .75", 1991.

Gatherer of Melons, fabricated and stamped, sterling silver, boulder opal and chrysocholla druse, 5.25" x 2.5" x 1", 1991.

Gift of the Eye Flower, fabricated and stamped, sterling silver, chrysoberyl and pearls, 4" x 1.5" x .5", 1991.

Photo credit: Ralph Gabriner

Jennifer Stenhouse

Lullaby Fish, cast, fabricated and patinated, bronze, silver, pewter, copper, lens, wood, sand, and colored pencils, 9" x 7" x 2", 1991. Photo credit: Brian Poulter

Shoes: Art Statements

by Gaza Bowen

I have been making various types of footwear since 1967. In 1986 I removed the limitation of function from my work and since have been exploring shoes from a broader perspective. My sculptures examine the relationships between people and shoes. What kinds of messages do shoes give us? What do they tell us about the people who wear them, the society in which they were made? How does a designed/manufactured item communicate emotions, mores and/or expectations? How and why do we give shoes such powerful roles to play in our lives? How is the power expressed?

On one level my comments are about shoes themselves. My background and training in shoemaking, plus the years spent repairing shoes, have given me a large vocabulary from which to draw. My studies in the history of fashion and frequent visits to museum collections to sketch and photograph have exposed me to new languages. At this level, my work is very much about the appearance of shoes, their construction, their connection to historical periods, and their function.

On another level my comments are about the social connotations and cultural symbolism with which shoes are imbued. Shoes are quite adept at expressing status, power, masculinity, femininity, mortality and spirituality. At this level I am concerned with the psychological function that shoes fulfill.

My selection and use of materials are integral to the communication of my ideas. Often I use materials that evoke specific responses based on their cultural and psychological associations. I have used metal in strategic places for both strength and psychological clout whenever necessary.

The strength of metal compared to its thinness makes it especially useful in creating non-visible supports and armatures.

Until recently most of the metal in my work was of this nature — hidden, but necessary. Occasionally I used metal for its messages, like knife blades for stiletto heels or turkey skewers for a strap closure. In these instances the metal object was chosen because its inherent message further communicated my intent — cold and shiny, or hard and mean. Recently I have been building pieces exclusively of metal with very different intentions.

In my many walks around the streets of Santa Cruz, I began picking up small pieces of squashed metal, mostly bottle caps, but also rusted cans, gaskets, wire, flattened paint tubes, aluminum turkey roasting pans, hub caps; really anything that attracted me and was light enough to carry home. The pieces shared certain qualities, a beauty of sorts, combined with a feeling of abandonment — remnants of function beneath layers of misuse. I wasn't sure how they related to shoes, but I did feel their relationship to people. each piece commented on my society.

After two years or so of collecting I began to get a feeling of what I wanted to make. But I had no idea how. I knew I didn't want to make a shoe and just cover it with all this stuff. I wanted the found object to be used in the actual structure of the shoe; the materials integral to the construction. As I piled things around and tried to find a way of fashioning a shoe-like object, I remembered that shoes are not solid, they are empty objects, containers really, I had to use my materials as a skin, to create an empty form. The moment I realized this I was only seconds away from solving the problem.

The two pieces illustrated here are the results of my recent experiments with metal. In both pieces the metal fragments are drilled and tacked together using shoe tacks. I can't imagine a simpler or more direct technique. *CASTE OFF* is a single boot, the type you would see in a littered alley up against a trash can. The sole is flapping, eyelets are missing and broken, the remnant of a frayed shoe lace remains.

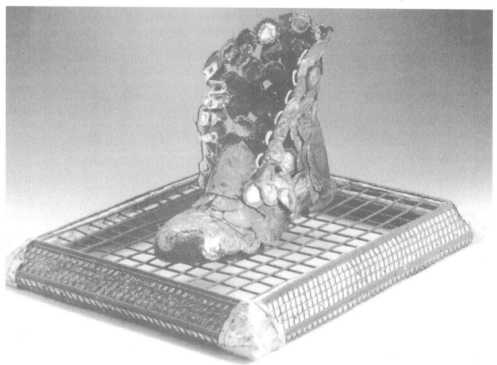

Caste Off, drilled and tacked, bottle caps, pull tabs, cans, wire and wood, 14" x 17" x 11",1992.

Article photo credit: Michael Kirkpatrick

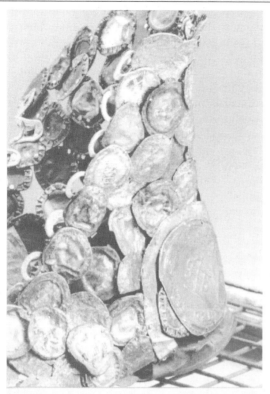

Caste Off, detail, 1992.

ing part of the hub cap. Signs of movement and speed are scraped into the hub cap's surface along with a sprinkling of broken windshield glass.

In these instances metal can do what no other material could. It is structurally light weight and thin, but strong enough to be both armature and skin. Its surface retains traces of its past. It both receives and reflects the touch of the human hand. I feel that I am just beginning to explore the potential of metal.

I have been a maker of things most of my life. My work began to have a focal point in 1976 when I participated in a two month intensive study of Colonial Shoemaking. I have taught at San Francisco State University and presented workshops throughout the U.S. In my Santa Cruz studio I teach small classes in functional shoemaking.

Its "pedestal," constructed of rusted grating, refers back to its niche in society, a place of diminished value. The boot is constructed of rusted bottle caps, can lids, pull tabs and wire. Each found object refers to specific shoe part — counter, backstay, eyelet, etc.

MEAN STREETS is also a single shoe — a white high top sneaker constructed of white and black bottle caps, can lids, a gas furnace filter, aluminum pull tabs and pop cans. Here the feeling of abandonment is combined with a sense of violence. The shoe is pressed into, almost becom-

Mean Streets, drilled and tacked, bottle caps, hub cap, wire, conduit, glass, paint, can lids and cans, 18" dia, 1992.

Patricia Fisher

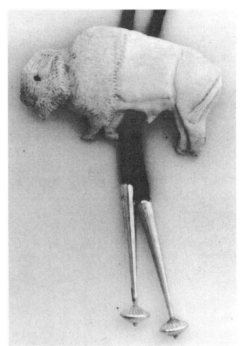

White Buffalo, Western America Series, carved, bone, leather, sterling and stone, 3" x .25" x 1.75", 1992

Western Jack Rabbit, Western America Series, repousse, patinated and carved, copper, bone and stone, 2" x .5" x 3.75", 1992.

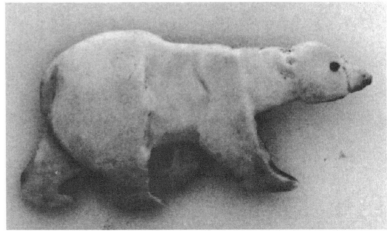

Arctic Bear, Pacific Rim Series, bone and stone, 2.5" x 1" x 1.5", 1992.

Richard Polsky

Untitled, roller printed, riveted and patinated, sterling silver, 1.25" x 2", 1992.

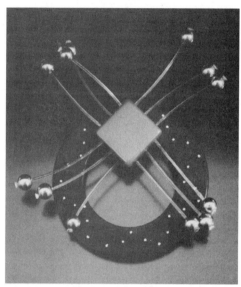

Untitled, riveted, epoxy, sterling silver, plastic, monofilament and bronze beads, 4" x 4" x 4", 1991.

Untitled, epoxy, wood toothpicks, dye, plastic and sterling silver, 3.5" x 1" x 1", 1991.

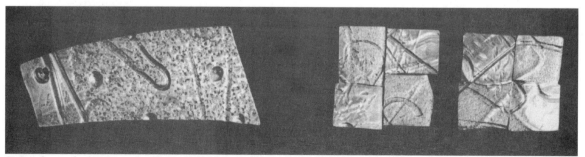

Brooch and earrings, roller printed, sterling silver, brooch: 2" x 1", earrings: .75" x .75", 1991.

Kim Eric Lilot

Manic-Depressive Ring, cast, chased and engraved, 18k gold, ring size, 1990.

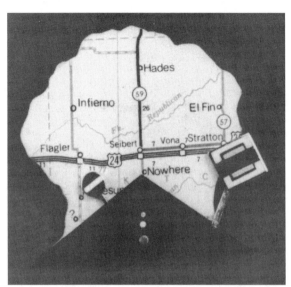

Road to Nowhere - 1990, brooch, fabricated and enamelled, slate, silver, 14k and 18k gold and map, 2" x 2" x 2", 1990.

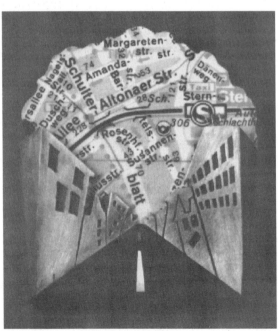

Road to Nowhere/Hamburg 1991, brooch, fabricated and cast, slate, 14k gold, silver and map, 2" x 2" x 2", 1991 (Depicts my environment and home during my German apprenticeship.)

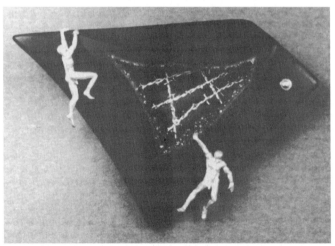

Escape - 1958, brooch, fabricated and cast, 18k gold, platinum and black druzy onyx (Pieter Lorenz carved), 2.25" x 1.5" x .5", 1991. (Depicts a childhood orphanage escape.)

Alice Van de Wetering

Circle of Life, reticulated, sterling, clay, amber, bone, wood and pre-columbian bead, 3.5" dia, 1991. Photo credit: Ralph Gabriner

Ancient Tale, reticulated, carved acrylic and sterling, 2.5" x 1.5", 1990. Photo credit: Stuart Mcallum

Lyn Licay

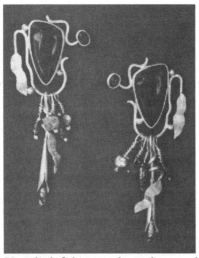

Untitled, fabricated, sterling and fine silver, black onyx, tourmalines, freshwater pearls and gemstone nuggets, 2.5" x 1", 1992.

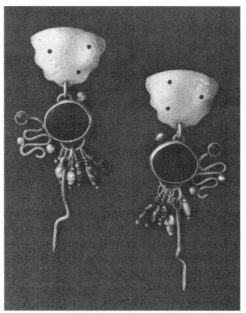

Untitled, fabricated, sterling and fine silver, river rocks, iolite and freshwater pearls, 2.75" x 1", 1991.

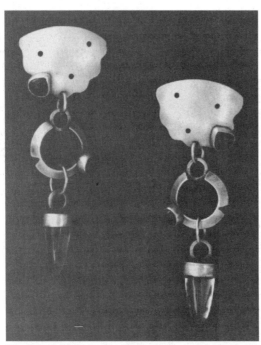

Untitled, fabricated, sterling and fine silver, tourmalines, amethyst and beryl, 2.5" x 1", 1990.

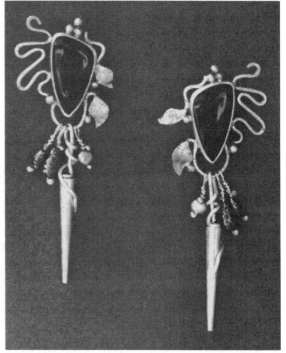

Untitled, fabricated, sterling and fine silver, black onyx and freshwater pearls, 2.75" x 1.25", 1992.

Photo credit: Stephen Heyer

Harold Gee
Holly Nelson Gee

Holly Nelson Gee, Untitled, Collage Series, fabricated, sterling silver and freshwater pearls, .75" x 2.5", 1992.

Harold Gee, Untitled, constructed, sterling silver, necklace: 26" x .5", earrings: 1.5" x .5", 1991.

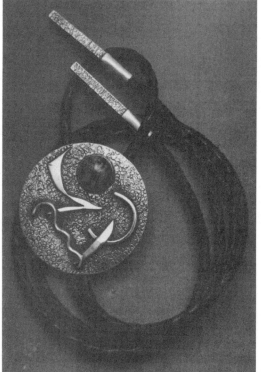

Holly Nelson Gee, Untitled, Scrappliqué Series, fabricated, sterling silver, snowflake obsidian and leather, 36" x 1.75", 1991.

Photo credit: Harold Gee

Peggy R. Cochran
Eleni Prieston

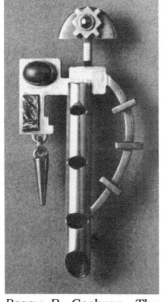

*Peggy R. Cochran, The Whistler, brooch, formed and constructed, sterling and fine silver, bronze, brass and malachite, 2.25" x 1.25", 1992.**

Eleni Prieston, Greek Coin Ring, cast, 18k and sterling, .75"dia, 1990.

*Peggy R. Cochran, Arched Drops, earrings, formed and carved, sterling silver, 2.25" x .5", 1992.**

Eleni Prieston, Opal Necklace, fused, fabricated and granulated, 22k, opal, ruby and tsavorite garnets, 18" chain, 1991.

*Photo credit: Harold Gee

Diane Archer

Personal Power, etched, marriage of metals and set stones, copper, nickel, bronze, brass, wood, tiger eye, obsidian, leather and found objects, 19" x 7" x 2", 1990. Photo credit: Robert Yost

Pendants, hollow formed, etched and stamped, sterling silver, bronze and leather, 3.5" x 1.75" x .5", 1991-92.*

Hope Deferred, etched, anodized and stamped, sterling silver, acrylic and aluminum, 22" x 5" x 1", 1991.*

*Photo credit: Robert ONeil

Displaying Jewelry

by Kris Patzlaff

Displaying jewelry can often present a more difficult problem than making jewelry. Showing work in local art exhibitions or those places (restaurants, banks, etc.) that provide local art groups and artists with exhibition space is usually impossible for jewelers. Many opportunities are also available in public buildings for displaying art, but are often restricted to wall space, again limiting access to jewelry artists. Another problem is the position of the work. Brooches or necklaces with parts meant to hang freely and earrings are often laid down on a flat surface, causing them to lose their power — compared to being displayed in a way closely resembling how they would be worn. Confronting a brooch or earrings at eye level is much more effective then leaning over a case and looking down on a piece.

Earrings, bone and sterling silver, 2" x 1", 1992. Photo credit and copyright 1992 J. Patrick Cudahy

Each person must decide for themselves how safety conscious they will be. This article shows one artist's approach to their own studio work. Do not follow it verbatim -- decide for yourself on the important issues of health and safety. See page 3.

214

The information in this article will help jewelry artists deal with some of these issues. Although not all jewelry may utilize these solutions, they may inspire other solutions to display problems that are unique to your own work.

The Display System

This display system is for displaying brooches, earrings and necklaces on the wall. Variations on one basic design will allow you to use this system in different ways, depending on the space you are showing in and the work to be shown.

The 3 Basic Components

1. Acrylic Box: This display system starts with an acrylic box that's open on one side. Acrylic photo boxes, widely available in photo and discount stores, are easily obtainable. They range in size from 4" x 6" to 30" x 40". These boxes are produced by many different manufacturers and are often repackaged by the store. <u>Do not</u> use the photo boxes that have a slight purple tinge to the acrylic when tilted in the light. This color becomes more evident when using it for display under lighting. Also note the depth of the box. This will vary with manufacturer. Choose the proper size box for your work. Be sure it gives your work ample space. Shop around as prices can vary significantly.

2. Mat Board: The mat board in this display system is used as a background and as a framing device. Choosing the color and size of the mat board in relationship to the size of the box is a personal decision. A wide range of colors are available at your local art store. Choose a color that best presents your work. The size of the mat board may create a border with as little as 1" extending from the sides of the acrylic box. Play with different sizes to see how much border works best for your

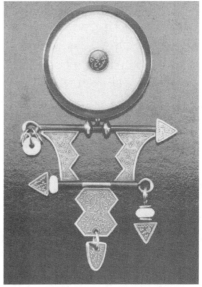

Brooch, bone and sterling silver, 3.5" x 2", 1992. Photo credit and copyright 1992 J. Patrick Cudahy

work, the size of your box and the exhibition space. Decide on the proper color and size. Cut, or have the art store cut the mat board.

3. 1/8" acrylic sheet: The size of this acrylic sheet is determined by the inside measurement of the acrylic box. Acrylic sheet may be purchased at glass or plastic supply shops. See your local phone directory for suppliers. Again, shop around as prices vary. Plastic suppliers tend to be the least expensive and their cutting costs minimal. Determine the correct size for the acrylic box you're working with and have the supplier cut it for you. The corners of the acrylic sheet will need to be rounded in order to fit inside of the acrylic box. Sand corners. (See about sanding in *Techniques and Tips* section of this article.)

At this point we must consider variations to accommodate different types of jewelry. The piece of 1/8" acrylic sheet will be fashioned in different ways to display the jewelry pieces. Some technical information needs to be covered before completing the display.

Techniques & Tips
for Working with Acrylic

1. Fusing acrylic: It is important that the surfaces to be fused are clean of grease and dust and that they fit flush. The bonding agent used for fusing is available at most hardware stores (in the glue section) and plastic supply shops. READ ALL DIRECTIONS on the product before using. This product is a health hazard. Follow all protective measures stated by manufacturer. This bonding agent actually breaks down the surface of the acrylic. Do not drip on the acrylic sheet as it will scar. Using a jeweler's third hand will be helpful when fusing small parts.

2. Bending acrylic: Bending acrylic sheet and rod is accomplished by heating the acrylic. This is done with a heat strip or heat gun. Again, READ ALL DIRECTIONS and follow all health and safety procedures stated by the manufacturer of this equipment. Work patiently. The acrylic need only to soften enough to bend it. Do not overheat. Heat only the areas that are to be bent, working one bend at a time. After bending to the appropriate shape, hold it there until it cools. When bending acrylic rod it is helpful to work with a larger piece

Earrings, bone and sterling silver, 2" x 1", 1992. Photo credit and copyright 1992 J. Patrick Cudahy

and then cut off the size you need. Practice on scraps to get a feel for this process.

3. Drilling acrylic: Acrylic may be drilled with steel drill bits. However, care must be taken when drilling. Do not allow the acrylic to heat up. If heated, your drill bit will become fused to the acrylic. A slow drill speed -and- frequently backing out of the hole when drilling, will help keep this from happening. Clean the drill bit often. CAUTION! Acrylic particle produced during drilling are an irritant. Wear all protective face gear including respirator and eye protection. READ ALL DIRECTIONS and follow all health and safety procedures as stated by the manufacturer of the tools and machinery you use.

4. Cutting acrylic: A preferred method of cutting acrylic sheet is by scoring and snapping. This process is done in the same way you would cut glass except that scoring is done with a razor knife instead of a glass cutter. I suggest you have the supplier cut the 1/16" acrylic sheet. The 1/16" acrylic sheet and acrylic rod can be worked easily. The acrylic rod may be scored with a file and snapped.

5. Sanding acrylic: Sanding of acrylic sheet and rod is done under water using wet and dry silicon carbide papers. Working with papers form 320 to 600 will provide a smooth finish. A polished finish may be accomplished by following 600 paper with tripoli and rouge. Apply polishing compounds to a buff stick. Do not use motorized buffing equipment.

6. Protective papers: Do not remove any of the protective papers or packaging form the acrylic until you are ready to use it. Do all measuring for drilling on protective paper. Keep paper on when sanding the edges of acrylic sheet. Peel back paper to expose only the area needed during fusing. All of these measures will help reduce the amount of scratches on the acrylic.

7. Have all parts for assembling within reach.

8. Remember to read and follow all guidelines by the tool and product manufacturer concerning safety, health and tool usage.

This mark (*) will appear throughout the remainder of this article to draw attention to areas where referral back to this *Techniques and Tips* section is advised.

Creating Devices
to Hold Jewelry in Display

The following are different devices for different types of jewelry. All of these devices are attached to the 1/8" acrylic sheet. The arrangement of these devices on the acrylic sheet and their size may vary according to the piece or pieces to be displayed. Measurements are given only as a suggestion.

1. Device for Earrings:

Materials: One piece of 1/16" acrylic sheet.

Process: Cut* the 1/16' acrylic sheet to measure 1 1/2" by 2 1/2". Measure, mark and drill* two holes with a #60 drill bit.

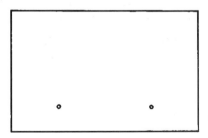

Bend* the acrylic sheet lengthwise to a 90° angle.

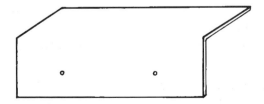

Fuse* the bent piece of acrylic to the 1/8" acrylic sheet.

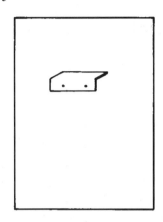

Attaching the earrings: Earring wires or posts are put through the drilled holes. Use the earring back to secure post earring.

2. Device for earrings:

Materials: Piece of 1/8" acrylic rod.

Process: Cut* a 4" length of acrylic rod. Drill* a hole with a #60 drill bit in the acrylic rod 1 1/2" from one end. Drill* a second hole 1 1/2" from the other end so that it lines up with the first hole.

Bend* the acrylic rod 3/4" from each end. Bend* one at a time to a 90° angle. Holes should be at the front of the "U" shaped acrylic rod.

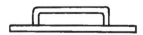

Sand* the cut edges smooth so that they fit flush to the surface of the 1/8" acrylic sheet.

Fuse* the acrylic rod to the acrylic sheet so it best accommodates the earrings to be shown.

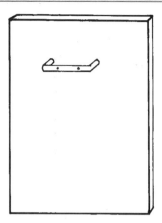

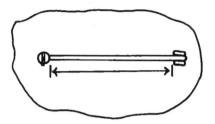

Add 1/8" to this measurement. Using an epoxy glue, secure the screw eyes into the holes.

Attaching the earrings: Earrings attach in the same manner as with device #1.

3. Device for Brooches:

Materials: Screw eyes: screw eyes are available from any jewelry supply company that sells findings. Their traditional use is for gluing into half drilled gem balls, etc. They are available in different sizes and plating colors. Choose whichever works best with the work to be shown.

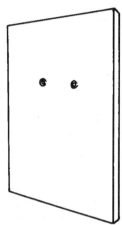

Allow drying time as indicated by the type of glue being used.

Attaching the brooch: Brooch is attached by putting the pin stem through the eyes on the acrylic sheet. Secure pin stem into the catch.

4. Device for Brooches: Ideal for fibulas and 3-D pieces.

Materials: 1/8" acrylic rod.

Process: Cut* two pieces of acrylic rod that best accommodates the brooch's thickness. Drill* a hole through the acrylic rod 1/8" from one end. Do this to both pieces.

Process: Choose a drill bit that matches the diameter of the screw eyes stem. Measure, mark and drill* two holes into the 1/8" acrylic sheet.

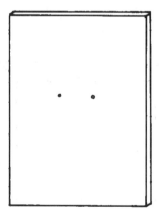

The space between the two holes is determined by the length of the pin stem on the brooch to be displayed. Measure the pin stem of the brooch while in a closed position, between the hinge and catch.

Use a drill bit that is larger than the diameter of the pin stem of the brooch to be displayed. Sand* the opposite ends so that they will fit flush to the 1/8" acrylic sheet. Sand* the ends with the drilled holes to finish. Fuse* the rods to the acrylic sheet.

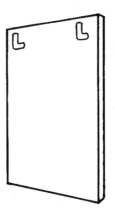

The space between the rods is determined by the length of the pin stem on the brooch to be displayed. Measure the pin stem of the brooch while in the closed position, between the catch and hinge.

Attaching the necklace or bolo: Necklace or bolo hangs over acrylic rods as shown.

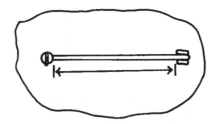

Add 3/8" to this measurement.

Attaching the brooch: Brooch is attached in the same manner as in device #3.

5. Device for Necklaces or Bolos:

Materials: 1/8" acrylic rod (a larger diameter may be needed for heavier work).

Process: Cut* the acrylic rod into two pieces measuring 1" in length. Bend* the acrylic rods to a 90° angle at 3/8" from one end.

Sand* and finish both ends of the rod. The end of the rod on the short side of the angle should fit flush against the acrylic sheet.

Fuse* the short end of the rod to the acrylic sheet in the corners.

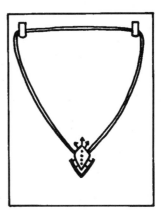

Assembling the Components

At this point you have three parts of the system ready to assemble.

1. The acrylic box.

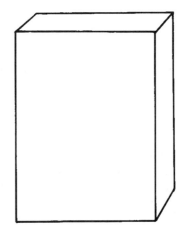

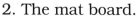

2. The mat board.

3. The acrylic sheet with the chosen device in place.

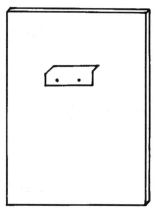

There are different solutions to assembling the components depending on the situation in which they are to be used.

1. Situation: On the wall display, okay to put significant holes in the wall, minimal security needed (artist is present), want work to be readily accessible.

Solution: Process: drill* two holes into the 1/8" acrylic sheet.

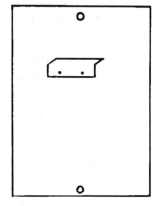

Place acrylic sheet in the center of the mat board.

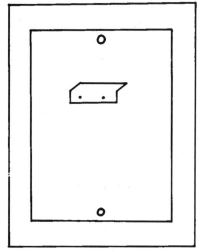

Mark the mat board to correspond with the holes in the acrylic. Using an awl make two holes in the mat board where its been marked. Note: Choose drill bit size to correspond with the screws to be used. Type and size of screw is determined by the size of the display, the weight of the piece being displayed and the type of wall the display will be fastened to. Larger displays may require drilling holes at each of the four corners of the acrylic sheet for added strength.

To assemble: First place the screws through the holes of the acrylic sheet, then through the holes in the mat board and then fasten to the wall.

Put jewelry in place. Acrylic box will then friction fit over the acrylic sheet. Line up the acrylic box on one side first and lightly pull out other side and push down to

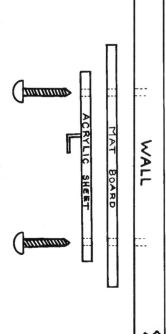

fit snugly. Note: You may decide to use this display without the acrylic box.

2. Situation: On the wall display, okay to put significant holes into wall, security is needed, do not need access to work.

Solution: Read and follow the process stated for #1. However, the acrylic box will be changed to provide the needed security.

Materials: Mirror clips. These can be purchased at the hardware store in many different styles. Choose the style that has a 90° angle.

Process: Cut* the mirror clip in half.

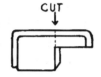

Take the piece with the hole in it (save left over piece) and sand* the rough edge flat. Take the acrylic box and fuse* the altered mirror clips to the sides of the acrylic box.

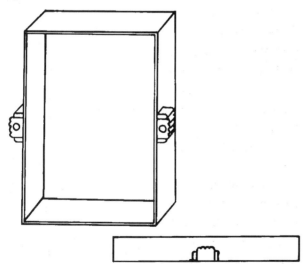

Work on a flat surface. Line up the holes in the acrylic sheet with the holes in the mat board. Place the acrylic box over the acrylic sheet and mat board. Mark the mat board to correspond with the altered mirror clip holes. Using an awl make holes in the mat board.

To assemble: First place screws through the holes of the acrylic sheet, then through the holes in the mat board and then fasten to the wall. Put jewelry in place. Place other screws through the holes of the altered mirror clips, then through the holes in the mat board and then fasten to wall.

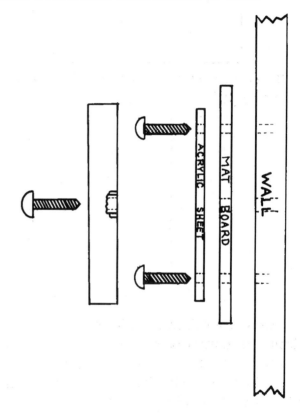

Note: For large acrylic boxes it may be necessary to attach additional mirror clips to the sides of the box.

3. Situation: On the wall display, minimal holes allowed in wall, relatively secure, do not need access to work.

Solution: Read and follow the process stated in #2. You may want to omit the drilled holes in the acrylic sheet since the wall cannot be used to secure the display. However the holes allow different options with one display.

Materials: The left over piece of the mirror clip from #2.

Process: Sand* the rough edge of the left over piece of the mirror clip smooth and flat. Take the acrylic box and place on end so that the open side is toward you. Fuse* the piece of mirror clip to the inside of the acrylic box 1/8" from the edge and in the middle.

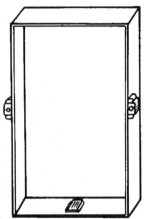

Turn the box around and do the same to the other end. Note: This will keep your acrylic sheet from falling forward in the acrylic box for this display solution. With larger sheets of acrylic and heavier pieces of jewelry more than two of these would be advisable.

To assemble: Use nuts and bolts to assemble. Put jewelry in place on the acrylic sheet and fit into the acrylic box. Place the bolts through the holes of the altered mirror clips and then through the mat board. Attach nuts to bolts to secure.

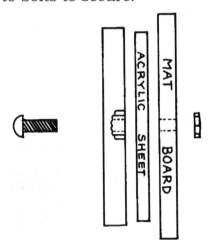

Use picture hanging wire attached to the back as the hanging device.

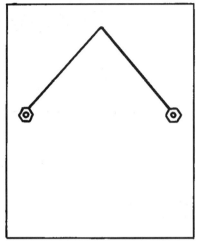

Hand on wall in the same manner you would a picture frame.

This display system can provide jewelry artists with many alternatives for displaying their work. With careful handling and protective storage, these displays can be used over and over again.

Copyright 1992 Kris Patzlaff

Kris Patzlaff holds an M.F.A. from Southern Illinois Univ., Carbondale and a B.A. from Humboldt State Univ., Arcata, CA. She exhibits her work nationally and is represented by numerous galleries. She has been working in the metals field for almost 20 years and has been an instructor at the Richmond Art Center.

LaPlantz Studios
Publications/Videos/Slides

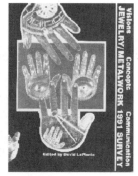

<u>Jewelry/Metalwork 1991 Survey</u> This is last year's Survey. With a similar format, it features 150 artist's work in 459 b/w photos and 17 articles. 160 pages. $19.95 + s/h.

<u>Artists Anodizing Aluminum: The Sulfuric Acid Process</u>: by David LaPlantz. This lavishly illustrated book has clear step-by-step instructions, diagrams and photos. 200 pages (8 in full color), soft bound, $19.95 + s/h.

Videos: These 3 videos by David LaPlantz include a blitz of visual and creative ideas/images/etc. Demonstrations, slide shows and ? VHS only.

Anodizing Aluminum Workshop: 1 hr 57 min, $29.95 + s/h (as a set with the book, $45.50)
Chain Mail/Chain Mesh: The Semi-solid Construction: 2 hrs, $29.95 + s/h
Cold Connections: 2 hrs, $29.95 + s/h

Slide Kits: These slide kits were part of a monthly slide service we used to offer. Each kit contains 5 - 35mm color slides of a single artist's work, the slide information, an artist's statement and bio. $4.50/ea, ppd. Send an SASE for a listing of artists still available. (They're going fast.)

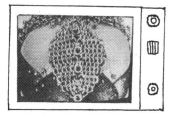

To order, ask questions, or to send an SASE for submission guidelines for next year's Survey, write or call:

David LaPlantz
PO Box 220
Bayside, CA 95524
800-845-6870

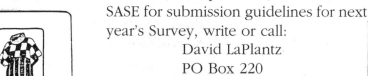

223

Index